Improve Your Chess

HARRY GOLOMBEK, OBE

*International Chess-Master and
British Chess Champion, 1947, 1949 and 1955*

Pitman Publishing

First published in Great Britain by Museum Press Limited as
"Instructions to Young Chess Players", 1958
Reprinted 1960
Reprinted 1966
Second revised and enlarged edition 1976

Pitman Publishing Ltd
Pitman House, Parker Street, Kingsway, London WC2B 5PB

Sir Isaac Pitman and Sons Ltd
PO Box 46038, Banda Street, Nairobi, Kenya

Pitman Publishing Pty Ltd
Pitman House, 158 Bouverie Street, Carlton, Victoria 3053,
Australia

Pitman Publishing Corporation
6 East 43rd Street, New York, NY 10017, USA

Pitman Publishing
Copp Clark Publishing
517 Wellington Street West, Toronto 135, Canada

ISBN 0 273 00066 7

Text set in 11/12 pt. Monotype Baskerville, printed by photo-
lithography, and bound in Great Britain at The Pitman Press,
Bath

G4556:14

CONTENTS

CHAPTER I

INTRODUCTORY

THE game of chess is such a fine one that it would be a pity not to play it as well as you can. This book is intended to help you improve your chess so that you can understand the game better, see more of its possibilities and enjoy it to the full. Incidentally, you should also win more games, which will automatically contribute to your pleasure in play. I cannot promise you will become world champions—the Alekhines and Capablancas, Botvinniks and Fischers are rare birds that come only once or twice in a century; but there is no reason at all why, with a little study on the lines of this book and good practice, you should not develop into a strong player, provided that you have normal human intelligence.

I have assumed as my starting-point that you know the moves and very little more. Those of you who do know rather more (say, chess terms and the notations) can skip the first two chapters; but, whatever your knowledge and strength as a player, please do not neglect the chapter on the endings which I know from experience to be a vital point in the make-up of any good player, let alone master player.

One further remark before I get down to business: do not be discouraged by early losses. Take on the strongest players you can find—the better they are the better your practice and the quicker you will improve.

THE NOTATIONS

The Descriptive (or English) Notation

The chess-board is made up of eight ranks and eight files, a rank being a row of eight squares running horizontally from left to right and a file being a vertical row of eight squares. Each file is named after the piece which originally stands on the first square of that file and each piece is represented by its first letter, with the exception of the Knight, which is represented by Kt. The squares in the file are numbered from one to eight, starting from bottom to top. The Rook, Bishop and Knight to the left of the Queen are called the QR, QB and QKt, respectively and those to the right of the King are called the KR, KB and KKt.

In Diagrams 1 and 2 are shown the names and numbers of each square, Diagram 1 being the board viewed from the White point of view, Diagram 2 being the board seen from Black's point of view. Thus, each square has two names, according to whether you are regarding the board from the White or the Black standpoint.

1

QR8	QKt8	QB8	Q8	K8	KB8	KKt8	KR8
QR7	QKt7	QB7	Q7	K7	KB7	KKt7	KR7
QR6	QKt6	QB6	Q6	K6	KB6	KKt6	KR6
QR5	QKt5	QB5	Q5	K5	KB5	KKt5	KR5
QR4	QKt4	QB4	Q4	K4	KB4	KKt4	KR4
QR3	QKt3	QB3	Q3	K3	KB3	KKt3	KR3
QR2	QKt2	QB2	Q2	K2	KB2	KKt2	KR2
QR1	QKt1	QB1	Q1	K1	KB1	KKt1	KR1

The Squares named from
White's point of view

2

QR1	QKt1	QB1	Q1	K1	KB1	KKt1	KR1
QR2	QKt2	QB2	Q2	K2	KB2	KKt2	KR2
QR3	QKt3	QB3	Q3	K3	KB3	KKt3	KR3
QR4	QKt4	QB4	Q4	K4	KB4	KKt4	KR4
QR5	QKt5	QB5	Q5	K5	KB5	KKt5	KR5
QR6	QKt6	QB6	Q6	K6	KB6	KKt6	KR6
QR7	QKt7	QB7	Q7	K7	KB7	KKt7	KR7
QR8	QKt8	QB8	Q8	K8	KB8	KKt8	KR8

The Squares named from
Black's point of view

A move is shown by giving the symbol for the piece and the name of the square to which that piece goes. Thus P—K4 means that the pawn on the King two square goes to the fourth square in that file. Captures are indicated by a ×. Thus P × P means pawn captures pawn and B × Q means Bishop takes Queen. If more than one pawn can make a capture, then the pawn in particular is shown by adding the symbol of the piece after which the file is named; thus KP × QP means the pawn on the King's file takes the pawn on the Queen's file. Similarly, when there is any doubt as to whether the Queen's Rook, Bishop or Knight rather than the King's Rook, Bishop or Knight made a move the Q or K is added accordingly. Castling is indicated in two ways: by the word Castles with the addition of K or Q if it is necessary to show whether the player castled Queen-side or King-side; or by o—o for King-side castling and o—o—o for Queen-side castling. A capture *en passant* is shown by the first letter of each word, thus P × P e.p. and check is abbreviated to ch.

To illustrate this, here is a game from the 1956 Scottish Championship:

FRENCH DEFENCE

White: P. B. Anderson. *Black:* M. Fallone

1. P—K4
(White plays pawn from K2 to K4.)
1. .... P—K3
(Black plays pawn from K2 to K3.)
2. P—Q4
(The White pawn goes from Q2 to Q4.)
2. .... P—Q4
(The Black pawn goes from Q2 to Q4.)
3. Kt—QB3
(Knight from QKt1 to QB3.)
3. .... Kt—KB3
(Knight from KKt1 to KB3.)
4. B—Kt5
(Bishop from QB1 to KKt5; note that this cannot be the King's Bishop since the move would also then include check and read B—Kt5 ch.)
4. .... B—K2
(Bishop from KB1 to K2.)
5. P—K5
(Pawn from K4 to K5.)
5. .... KKt—Q2
(Knight from KB3 to Q2; it is necessary to add K as the QKnight could also go to Q2.)
6. P—KR4
(Pawn from KR2 to KR4.)
6. .... P—KR3
(Pawn from KR2 to KR3.)
7. B × B
(Bishop captures Bishop.)
7. .... Q × B
(Queen takes Bishop.)

8. P—B4
(Pawn from B2 to B4.)

8. ....   P—R3
(Pawn from QR2 to QR3; it is no longer necessary to add Q as the KR pawn has already moved.)

9. Kt—B3
(Knight from KKt1 to KB3.)

9. ....   P—QB4
(Pawn from QB2 to QB4.)

10. Q—Q2
(Queen from Q1 to Q2.)

10. ....   Kt—QB3
(Knight from QKt1 to QB3.)

11. o—o—o
(Castles Queen-side.)

11. ....   P—QKt4
(Pawn from QKt2 to QKt4.)

12. B—K2
(Bishop from B1 to K2.)

12. ....   P—B5
(Pawn from QB4 to B5.)

13. P—KKt4
(Pawn from KKt2 to Kt4.)

13. ....   Kt—Kt3
(Knight from Q2 to QKt3.)

14. QR—Kt1
(Rook from Q1 to KKt1; note that it is necessary to state which Rook goes to Kt1.)

14. ....   P—Kt5
(Pawn from QKt4 to Kt5.)

15. Kt—Kt1
(Knight from QB3 to Kt1.)

15. ....   Kt—R5
(Knight from QKt3 to QR5.)

16. P—B3
(Pawn from QB2 to QB3.)

16. ....   R—QKt1
(Rook from QR1 to QKt1.)

17. Q—Q1
(Queen from Q2 to Q1.)

17. ....   Kt × KtP
(Knight from QR5 takes pawn on QKt7.)
18. K × Kt
(King from B1 takes Knight.)
18. ....   P × P db. ch
(Pawn on QKt5 takes pawn on QB6 giving check and
revealing check with the Rook.)
White resigns.
The final position is shown in Diagram 3.

3

Final Position

Algebraic Notation

In this notation each square has only one name, whether
looked at from White or from Black. The squares are numbered
from 1 to 8 in the file reading from bottom to top (with White
at the bottom) and the files are each indicated by a letter
a to *h* running from left to right (again from White's point of
view).

The symbols for the pieces are the same as in the descriptive
notation and o—o and o—o—o are always used for castling.
To represent a move, you add to the symbol for the piece the
name of the square it leaves and that of the square to which it
goes. In the case of a pawn, however, the symbol is omitted.
Thus e2—e4 is the equivalent of P—K4 and Ktb1—c3 is the
same as Kt—QB3.

There is also a shortened form of the algebraic in which
the name of the departure square is omitted, except in cases of
ambiguity.

Diagram 4 shows the chess-board numbered and lettered according to the algebraic notation.

4

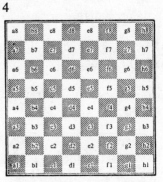

Algebraic notation

Here is the same game as above rendered first in the full algebraic notation and then in the abbreviated form:

1. e2–e4, e7–e6; 2. d2–d4, d7–d5; 3. Ktb1–c3, Ktg8–f6; 4. Bc1–g5, Bf8–e7; 5. e4–e5, Ktf6–d7; 6. h2–h4, h7–h6; 7. Bg5×e7, Qd8×e7; 8. f2–f4, a7–a6; 9. Ktg1–f3, c7–c5; 10. Qd1–d2, Ktb8–c6; 11. o–o–o, b7–b5; 12. Bf1–e2, c5–c4; 13. g2–g4, Ktd7–b6; 14. Rd1–g1, b5–b4; 15. Ktc3–b1, Ktb6–a4; 16. c2–c3, Ra8–b8; 17. Qd2–d1, Kta4×b2; 18. Kc1×b2, b4×c3 db. ch; White resigns.

1. e4, e6; 2. d4, d5; 3. Ktc3, Ktf6; 4. Bg5, Be7; 5. e5, Ktfd7; 6. h4, h6; 7. B×e7, Q×e7; 8. f4, a6; 9. Ktf3, c5; 10. Qd2, Ktc6; 11. o–o–o, b5; 12. Be2, c4; 13. g4, Ktb6; 14. Rdg1, b4; 15. Ktb1, Kta4; 16. c3, Rb8; 17. Qd1, Kt×b2; 18. K×b2, b×c db. ch; resigns.

The descriptive notation is used only in English-speaking countries and the algebraic everywhere else in the world. Which is the better? The algebraic is clearer in that there is one name for each square; it also occupies much less space, especially in the abbreviated form. On the other hand, when writing down a score it is very easy to confuse the *c* and the *e*.

Methods of taking down Positions

There are three of these. The simplest is when you have an empty diagram, when all that is necessary is to put down the symbols for the pieces in the appropriate squares, ringing round those that are Black and adding whose turn it is to move. Thus the final position in Diagram 3 would appear as in the diagram below. It is a useful precaution to put the number of Black

5   Black (14 pieces)

White (13 pieces)
White to play

pieces and the number of White pieces at the top and bottom of the diagram as I have done.

When you have not got a diagram handy, the Forsyth notation can be used. Looking at the board from left to right, starting with the top rank, the pieces are written down, represented by their normal symbols. White pieces are indicated by capitals and Black pieces by small letters. The number of vacant squares is noted and the end of a rank is indicated by a sloping stroke (or else by a semi-colon). Thus the position in Diagram 3 would appear in Forsyth as follows:

1 r b 1 k 2 r / 4 q p p 1 / p 1 kt 1 p 2 p / 3 p P 3 / 2 p P 1 P P P / 2 p 2 KT 2 / P K 2 B 3 / 1 KT 1 Q 2 R R.

The third method can be employed with the algebraic notation and then you simply note the pieces and the squares on which they stand. This can also be done with the descriptive notation but the fact that in the latter case each square has two names causes confusion. Thus in algebraic the position in Diagram 3 appears: Black: K on e8, Q on e7, R on b8 and h8, B on c8, Kt on c6, pawns on a6, c4, c3, d5, e6, f7, g7, h6. White: K on b2, Q on d1, Rook on g1 and h1, B on e2, Kt on f3 and b1, pawns on a2, d4, e5, f4, g4, h4.

CHAPTER II

CHESS TERMS

IN the course of time a number of terms have arisen in chess which it will be useful for you to know, since knowledge of what these terms mean will certainly help your play. Here they are in alphabetical order.

CHECK

"Discovered check" is given when one piece, in moving, uncovers the action of another on the King. Thus, in Diagram 1, the Bishop moves and thus allows the Queen to give discovered check. "Double check" is given when two pieces check the King at the same time. This is really only a special case of discovered check and only by discovering check can one give double check. In Diagram 2 White gives double check by playing either Kt—Q6 or Kt—B6.

6

7

Discovered Check   Double Check

Double check is the atomic bomb of the chess-board and nothing can withstand it. Look at the final move in the following game from the World Student Team Championship at Uppsala in 1956.

RUY LOPEZ

White: Pietsch.   *Black:* Lahti

1. P—K4, P—K4; 2. Kt—KB3, Kt—QB3; 3. B—Kt5, P—QR3; 4. B—R4, Kt—B3; 5. P—Q3, P—QKt4; 6. B—Kt3, P—Q3; 7. P—B3, B—K2; 8. o—o, Kt—QR4; 9. B—B2, P—B4; 10. QKt—Q2, Q—B2; 11. R—K1, o—o; 12. Kt—B1, Kt—B3; 13. Q—K2, P—Kt5; 14. B—Kt5, P—QR4; 15. QR—B1, Kt—Q2; 16. B—Q2, Kt—Kt3; 17. Kt—Kt3, B—K3; 18. B—Kt1, P—B3; 19. P—Q4, KtP×P; 20. KtP×P, B—B5; 21. Q—Q1, P—R5; 22. P—Q5, Kt—R2; 23. Kt—R4, KR—Kt1; 24. Q—Kt4, Q—Q2; 25. Kt(Kt3)—B5, B—B1; 26. R—K3, R—Kt2; 27. R—Kt3, K—R1; 28. Q—R5, Kt—Kt4; 29. Kt—Kt6 ch, K—Kt1; 30. Kt—R6 ch, P×Kt; 31. Kt—K7 db. ch, resigns.

CENTRE

The centre is made up of the four central squares on the board, White's K4 and Q4, and Black's K4 and Q4. It is the most important section of the board since the player in control of these four squares can easily switch his forces in attack or defence in any direction.

COMBINATION

This is a sequence of moves that fit together to serve some particular purpose. The following brilliant little game can be regarded as containing a combination that starts with Black's seventh move and ends with his last. Or, if you are a suspicious sort of person and do not believe the winner saw right through to the end, then you may say that it contains two combinations, one starting with his seventh move, and one starting with his fifteenth.

GIUOCO PIANO, PHILADELPHIA, 1860

White: Amateur.   *Black:* Derrickson

1. P—K4, P—K4; 2. B—B4, Kt—KB3; 3. Kt—KB3, Kt—B3; 4. o—o, B—B4; 5. P—Q3, P—Q3; 6. B—KKt5, B—KKt5; 7. P—KR3, P—KR4; 8. P×B, P×P; 9. Kt—R2, P—Kt6; 10. Kt—KB3, Kt—KKt5; 11. B×Q, B×P ch; 12. R×B, P×R ch; 13. K—B1, R—R8 ch; 14. K—K2, R×Q; 15. KKt—Q2, Kt—Q5 ch; 16. K×R, Kt—K6 ch; 17. K—B1, Kt—K7 mate.

EN PRISE

To place a pawn or a piece *en prise* means to put it where it can be captured.

EXCHANGE

To win the exchange means to win a Rook of the opponent's in return for a Knight or a Bishop of one's own, so that the exchange in this instance really means the difference in value between a Rook and a Knight or a Rook and a Bishop.

FIANCHETTO

To *fianchetto* is to develop a Bishop either on KKt2 or on QKt2 after having advanced the Kt pawn one square. In the following opening both sides *fianchetto* all their Bishops: 1. P—KKt3, P—KKt3; 2. B—Kt2, B—Kt2; 3. Kt—KB3, Kt—KB3; 4. P—Kt3, P—Kt3; 5. B—Kt2, B—Kt2.

FORK

To fork is to attack two pieces at the same time with one piece. Thus, in Diagram 8, the White Knight is forking the Black Queen and Rook, whilst the Black pawn is forking the two White Rooks.

The fork is a deadly weapon that is used to gain material, as, for example, in Diagram 9, where Black played 31. .... R—Q7 ch; 32. K×R, Kt×P ch; 33. K—Q3, Kt×R; 34. Kt—B6 ch, K—B3; 35. Kt×P, P—Kt5; 36. Kt—B6, Kt—B6; 37. K—K2, Kt×P; 38. P—R4, P—Kt6; White resigns, the threat being P—B6 ch, whilst if 39. Kt—Q4, K—K4; 40. Kt—B3 ch, K×P.

8

The Fork

9   Black (Geller) to play

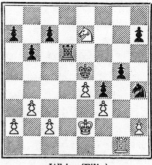

White (Filip)
Amsterdam, 1956

GAMBIT

To play a gambit is to sacrifice a pawn (or sometimes even a piece) in the opening in the hope of gaining an advantage either in development or in position or in both. Typical gambits are the King's Gambit: 1. P—K4, P—K4; 2. P—KB4, and the Evans Gambit: 1. P—K4, P—K4; 2. Kt—KB3, Kt—QB3; 3. B—B4, B—B4; 4. P—QKt4.

J'ADOUBE

This is French for "I adjust", and should be said before you touch a piece with the intention of adjusting it to its rightful position, the idea being that if a piece is placed half on one square, half on another and you want to put it on the right square then, in order to guard yourself against the rule of moving a touched piece you say "*J'adoube*".

MATE

Smothered Mate

When an opposing King is so choked up by its own pieces that you only need a Knight check to deliver mate then you give smothered mate. The usual example is in Diagram 10.

An amusing example of smothered mate in practical play is shown in Diagram 11. Black incautiously played 36. ...., Kt—Kt3; to which White replied 37. Kt—B6 mate.

10

Smothered Mate

11 Black (Winants) to play

White (Boey)
Belgian Championship, 1957

Philidor's Legacy

Or Philidor's mate is a special type of smothered mate which starts off with a Queen sacrifice. A beautiful example is shown in the following game:

TWO KNIGHTS' DEFENCE, PARIS, 1859

White: Morphy.   *Black:* Amateur

1. P—K4, P—K4; 2. Kt—KB3, Kt—QB3; 3. B—B4, Kt—B3;
4. P—Q4, P×P; 5. o—o, Kt×P; 6. R—K1, P—Q4; 7. B×P,
Q×B; 8. Kt—B3, Q—KR4; 9. Kt×Kt, B—K3; 10. Kt(K4)—
Kt5, B—QKt5; 11. R×B ch, P×R; 12. Kt×KP, Q—B2; 13.
Kt(B3)—Kt5, Q—K2; 14. Q—K2, B—Q3; 15. Kt×KtP ch,
K—Q2; 16. Q—Kt4 ch, K—Q1; 17. Kt—B7 ch, Q×Kt; 18.
B—Kt5 ch, B—K2; 19. Kt—K6 ch, K—B1; 20. Kt—B5 dis. ch,
K—Kt1; 21. Kt—Q7 ch, K—B1; 22. Kt—Kt6 db. ch, K—
Kt1; 23. Q—B8 ch, R×Q; 24. Kt—Q7 mate.

OPPOSITION

When the Kings are directly opposite one another, either
vertically, horizontally or diagonally, and as near as is legally
possible, then that side whose turn it is *not* to move is said to
have the opposition. For more about the opposition see
Chapter III, p. 24.

PAWNS

(a) Backward

A backward pawn is one that is a square behind its adjacent
pawns on either side as in the left-hand three pawns in Diagram
12. This is usually a disadvantage, since the pawn lacks support,
and in addition there is a troublesome hole on which an enemy
piece can settle itself.

(b) Doubled

When two pawns of the same colour are in the same file they
are called "doubled". Similarly, when three pawns of the same
colour are in the same file they are called "tripled", though this
is a much rarer case. In Diagram 12 the doubled pawns are
on the KR file.

(c) Hanging

When two adjacent pawns of the same colour and on the
same rank have no pawns of their own colour on the next files
on both sides they are called hanging pawns. Usually they are
to be found on the fourth rank, as are the pawns on K4 and
KB4 in Diagram 12.

12

(d) Isolated

An isolated pawn is one that has no pawn of its own colour on both adjacent files. Thus in Diagram 13 the White pawns on K4 and KKt5 and the Black pawn on Q2 are isolated. This is usually a disadvantage, as the pawn that is isolated lacks protection and can easily be captured.

(e) Passed

A passed pawn is one that has no enemy pawn capable of stopping its progress to the eighth rank, that is, a pawn that has no enemy pawn in the file directly in front or on the two adjacent files (again in front of the pawn). Thus, in Diagram 13 the White pawns on QR4, QKt5, and KKt5 and the Black pawn on KKt5 are passed. This is a great advantage, as it means that one of the main obstacles to queening a pawn has been removed. An even stronger type of passed pawn is the supported passed pawn as on QKt5 in Diagram 13.

13

PIECES

A major piece is a Queen or a Rook. A minor piece is a Knight or a Bishop.

PIN

A pin is when one attacks a piece so that it cannot move without allowing the attack to fall on a piece of still greater value, or, in the case when this piece of greater value is the King itself, so that it cannot move legally at all. Diagram 14 shows the two types of pins. Black's Knight cannot move at all, since the White Bishop pins it on the King. White's KKt can move, but only at the cost of losing the Queen, and this is also a severe pin.

The pin is a very useful method of attack which is to be found in many openings and also occurs often in the other phases of the game.

14

The Pin

SYMBOLS

Some signs and symbols have already been given in Chapter I, but here are a few more that are often seen:

! good move; ? bad move; = level game; + with the better game for White or Black, according to whether it is put after the White or Black move (this is also used in algebraic notation to signify check); ± with advantage to White; ∓ with advantage to Black; + + with a won game for White or Black, according to whether it is put after the White or Black move (this is also used in algebraic notation to signify checkmate);

: used sometimes in algebraic notation instead of × to indicate a capture.

ZUGZWANG

A German word meaning compulsion to move. This describes a situation in which a player has no good move and in which any move he makes results in loss of material or the game itself. *Zugzwang* is most often seen in the end-game, though it does also appear in the later stages of the middle-game. A typical end-game example is shown in Diagram 15. White plays 1. K—R4, and now Black is in *zugzwang*. He would be perfectly happy to do without his move, but as it is he must move his King away from the pawn and allow White to capture it.

15

White to Play

THE END-GAME

THIS is the phase of the game that is most neglected by young and old players alike—and yet this is the most important. Unless you are a good end-game player you will never get anywhere in the chess world. Without exception of any kind, I have always seen the good end-game player come out above the opening or middle-game specialist. It almost goes without saying that all the world's greatest players, both in the past and in the present have excelled in the endings and the 1972 World Champion, Bobby Fischer, was also a remarkably fine end-game player.

Players who are not interested in this part of the game usually advance two reasons for their lack of enthusiasm for the end-game: that it is dull and that it is difficult. Now, the first reason merely shows their failure to understand the endings. Just as much brilliance, just as much subtlety and just as much fun can be found in the end-game as in any other phase of chess, openings or middle-game. Just try studying the endings a little and you will be surprised how full of excitement and colour they are. As for difficulty—well, chess is a difficult game to play well, and again the endings are no more and no less difficult than the openings or the middle-game. Here, as always in chess, the main point is to understand what are the basic aims. Understanding plus practice will make you a good end-game player and, what is more, will enable you to enjoy the endings and therefore chess to the full.

This having been said let us have a look at the most basic type of ending of all.

THE PAWN ENDINGS

Here the main problem is how to force on the pawn to the eighth rank (though on the way you should not be averse to picking up a pawn or two when you get the chance). The final winning positions you should have in mind are shown in

Diagrams 16 and 17. In the first it does not matter who has the move, the white pawn simply checks its way to the eighth rank. In the second it is vital that it should be Black's turn to move for then comes 1. ...., K—K2; 2. K—B7, and the pawn queens; whereas if it is White's turn the game ends in a draw by 1. K—Q6, stalemate!

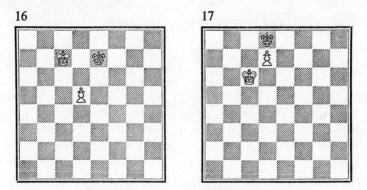

16   17

Naturally, if the pawn is far enough ahead, or far enough away, from the opposing King it can queen without any aid from its own King and there is a very simple way of working out whether it can do so (Diagram 18).

18

THE QUEENING SQUARE

You count the number of squares from the pawn to the queening square and make the shape of a square as in Diagram 18. If the opposing King is outside the square thus formed it cannot stop the pawn. If it is inside the square, then the pawn will be intercepted. In Diagram 18 it is clearly outside the square. Shift the King one square further to the left and White still wins if it is his turn to move. If it is Black's turn, however, he makes a move and enters the square.

This, then, is a useful method of making sure whether or not the enemy King can intercept your pawn; but now I come to something much more important which dominates the whole theory and practice of pawn endings.

THE OPPOSITION

You will remember that in the chapter on chess terms I said that when two Kings are directly opposite one another and as near as is legally possible then that side whose turn it is *not* to move is said to have the opposition. In Diagram 19 I show the three types of opposition, vertical, horizontal and diagonal.

19

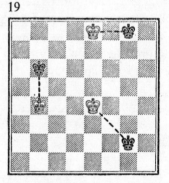

Now, what is the advantage in possessing the opposition? Well, imagine that you are walking along a narrow passage and you meet someone coming in the opposite direction. When you come up to him you are in the position of the two Kings on the chess-board. The laws of politeness forbid you to knock into him; so, the one of you who is first to move must take a step back to give way. So it is in chess: the King whose turn it is to move (i.e. the one that has not got the opposition) must give ground.

The opposition can thus be used to force the King away from the queening square; or, if you—the possessor of the pawn

—do not have the opposition, then it may well mean the win is impossible. Take the two positions on Diagram 20. In the left-hand position with White to move he plays 1. P—B7, and wins as in Diagram 17. In the right-hand position, with White to move, in order to get any further he must play 1. P—B7 ch, when 1. ...., K—B1; 2. K—B6, gives us the draw by stalemate. In this case Black draws because he has the opposition.

20

Make it Black's turn to move and the case is completely altered. White has the opposition and therefore wins, the game going 1. ...., K—B1; 2. P—B7, K—Kt2; 3. K—K7, and the pawn queens. From this emerges another useful little rule. When the opposing King is in front of either your King or your pawn you must be able to get your pawn to the seventh rank without delivering check with the pawn if you want to win.

Let us see how the opposition works when the pawn is a long way, as far as possible, from the queening square.

21

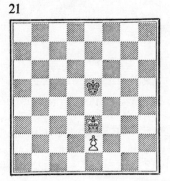

Here with Black to play (that is, with White having the opposition) White wins; with White to play (that is, with Black having the opposition) it is a draw.

Supposing it is Black to play White wins as follows: 1. ...., K—B4 (if 1. ...., K—Q4; 2. K—B4, and White wins by a similar process to that I now give); 2. K—Q4, K—K3; K—K4 (regaining the opposition, but now his King has forced back the opposing King one square); 3. ...., K—B3; 4. K—Q5, K—K2; 5. K—K5, K—B2; 6. K—Q6, K—K1; 7. K—K6, K—Q1; 8. P—K4, K—K1; 9. P—K5, K—B1; 10. K—Q7, K—B2; 11. P—K6 ch, followed by 12. P—K7 and 13. P—K8=Q.

Going back to Diagram 21 and supposing it is White to play, then 1. K—Q3, K—Q4; 2. P—K4 ch, K—K3; 3. K—Q4, K—Q3; 4. P—K5 ch, K—K2; 5. K—Q5, K—Q2; 6. P—K6 ch, K—K1; 7. K—Q6, K—Q1; 8. P—Q7 ch, K—K1; 9. K—K6, stalemate. Note that Black continually maintains his possession of the opposition and that, when he has to retreat, he does so by going to one square directly in front and away from the pawn.

The next position is perhaps the most instructive and typical of all. This is a win for White no matter whose turn it is to move, for the fact that his King is one square in front of his

22

pawn means that he always has a spare move with his pawn to gain the opposition. With White to move he wins by 1. P—K4, K—B2; 2. K—Q6, K—K1; 3. K—K6, and we are back in the line given as winning in Diagram 21. With Black to move the process is similar 1. ...., K—B2; 2. K—Q6, etc.

Another typical winning position is shown in Diagram 23. This is a win for White, whether he has the opposition or not to start off with, the point being that as the Black King is on the back rank it has less opportunity for manœuvring and so cannot maintain the opposition. With Black to move, White wins after 1. ...., K—Q1; 2. K—B7, etc., or 1. ...., K—B1; 2. K—Q7. With White to move, he wins by 1. K—Q6, K—Q1; (or 1. ...., K—B1; 2. K—Q7); 2. P—K6 (and now White has the opposition); 2. ...., K—K1; 3. P—K7, K—B2; 4. K—Q7.

23

All these positions and their possibilities, however, do not apply when a Rook pawn is concerned. If the Black King is on the Rook file in front of the pawn, it does not matter where the White King is or who has the opposition, the ending is drawn as the Black King cannot be edged out of the corner. In the left-hand position of Diagram 24 after 1. P—R4, K—Kt1; 2. P—R5, K—R1; 3. K—Kt6, K—Kt1; 4. P—R6, K—R1;

24

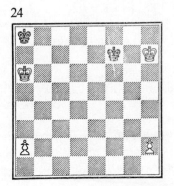

5. P—R7, it is stalemate. Or, with Black to play, 1. ....,
K—Kt1; 2. P—R4, K—R1; 3. P—R5, K—Kt1; 4. K—Kt6,
K—R1; 5. P—R6, K—Kt1; 6. P—R7 ch, K—R1; 7. K—R6,
stalemate.

The stalemate and the draw come in another way in the
right-hand position of Diagram 24. After 1. P—R4, K—B1;
2. P—R5, K—B2; 3. P—R6, K—B1; 4. K—R8 (or 4. K—Kt6,
K—Kt1, and the Black King gets to R1); 4. ...., K—B2;
5. P—R7, K—B1, stalemate.

With two pawns against a solitary King the win is much
easier, as White can always get one of the winning positions
given above by shedding one of the pawns at the right moment.

King and two pawns against King and one pawn usually
win, the exception being almost always where a Rook pawn is
concerned. Typical winning methods are shown in Diagrams
25 and 26. In the first case White wins by 1. K—K5, K—K1;

25

26

2. K—Q6, K—Q1; 3. P—Kt6, P×P; 4. P—B7. In the second
he wins by 1. K—Q5, K—K1 (or 1. ...., K—B3; 2. K—K4,
K—K2; 3. K—K5, K—K1; 4. K—K6, K—B1; 5. K—Q7,
and we are back in the main line); 2. K—K6, K—B1; 3.
K—Q7 (and not 3. P—B6, K—Kt1; 4. P—B7 ch, K—B1;
when the game is drawn); 3. ...., K—Kt1; 4. K—K7,
K—R1; 5. P—B6, and if (a) 5. ...., P×P; 6. K—B7, P—B4;
7. P—Kt7 ch, or (b) 5. ...., K—Kt1; 6. P—B7 ch, K—R1;
7. P—B8=Q, mate.

Before leaving the realm of pure pawn play, here is just one
more example of the power of the opposition from a tournament game. Here White having the move (and therefore

not having the opposition) resigned; for if 1. K—K3, K—B5; 2. K—Q2, K—Kt6, or if 1. K—Q2, K—K5.

27   Black (Hofmann)

White (Holzer) to play
Austrian Championship, 1957

PAWN (OR PAWNS) AGAINST PIECES

Against the Knight

Here it is the possessor of the Knight who is usually struggling to get the draw. A typical example of a drawing position is shown in Diagram 28. Though the White King is far away

28

and can give no aid to the Knight that solitary piece can force the draw by 1. Kt—B1 ch, K—Kt7; 2. Kt—Q3 ch, K—B7; 3. Kt—Kt4 ch, K—Kt6; 4. Kt—Q3, and the game is drawn since if 4. ...., P—R7; 5. Kt—B1 ch, and the Knight is given up for the pawn.

How helpless the Knight can be against a pawn is shown by the following ending:

29   Black (Donner)

White (Pilnik) to play
Beverwijk, 1958

White now won by 53. P—Kt5, P×P; 54. P×P, Kt—B3;
55. P—Kt6, Kt×P; 56. P—Kt7, Kt—K4 ch; 57. K—B7,
P—Kt4; 58. P—Kt8=Q, Kt—B6; 59. Q—Kt4, resigns.
This was a particularly tragic moment for the young Dutch
player Donner, as it took place in the last round of the
Beverwijk tournament, when all he needed to attain the
grandmaster title was another half-point.

Against the Bishop

The Bishop, which has a further reach than the Knight, is
usually better at dealing with pawns; but even the Bishop
may find it difficult to stop one of two passed pawns that are
widely apart. An example of this from a Soviet Championship tournament is shown in Diagram 30. Black now gives

30   Black (Tal) to play

White (Keres)
XXIV U.S.S.R. Championship, 1957

up his Bishop for two pawns so as to obtain two remotely distant passed pawns: 39. ...., B×P; 40. P×B, K×P; 41. K—B1, P—Kt4; 42. B—Q2 (stopping the KtP, but now the RP advances); 42. ...., P—R5; 43. B—Kt4, P—R6; 44. K—Kt1, K—K7; White resigns. For, after 45. K—R2, P—B5; 46. K×P, P—B6, either the BP or the KtP must queen.

A more complicated example (but with the same principle behind it) can be seen in Diagram 31. Here, though White is a

31   Black (Popov) to play

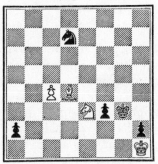

White (Bondarevsky)
Bulgaria, 1949

piece up, there are too many pawns for the Bishop to watch, whilst White's Knight is of very little use in controlling the distant passed pawns. Black wins by 1. ...., Kt—B4; 2. Kt—B1 ch, K—R6; 3. Kt×P (or 3. Kt—Q2, P—B7; 4. B—Kt2, Kt—K5); 3. ...., P—B7; 4. Kt—B1, Kt—K5; 5. B—K5, Kt—Kt6 ch; 6. Kt×Kt, P—R8=Q ch; 7. B×Q, K×Kt, and Black mates in three moves.

Against pawns that are close together, the Bishop is usually more successful; but even here there are some cases in which it is helpless, e.g. the position in Diagram 32, where White wins by 1. P—B7 ch, K—B1; 2. P—Kt7 ch, K×P; 3. K—R7, etc.; the manner in which the Black King and the Black Bishop get in each other's way is comic. Naturally, this is an exceptionable position; if, for instance, the Black Bishop were stationed anywhere along the diagonal QKt1—KR7 then there would be no question of a win for White.

32

White to play

Against the Rook

The Rook usually has little difficulty in dealing with pawns; the fact that they are distant from each other is no trouble for the Rook, which speeds down files and ranks to capture them. Yet there are certain known positions in which the Rook is helpless, the most important being when one side has two united passed pawns that have reached the sixth rank. Once the pawns have got so far, the Rook cannot hinder one or other of the pawns queening. Take the position in Diagram 33;

33

no matter whose turn it is to move, White cannot prevent one of the pawns from queening, e.g. 1. R—R7, P—Kt7; 2. R—QKt7, P—R7; equally, if 1. R—K3, P—Kt7; 2. R—QKt3, P—R7.

The other type of position is that in which the pawns (connected or otherwise) are far advanced and their King can aid them to queen whilst the opposing King is too far away to have any say in the matter. Such a position is that in Diagram 34. The game ended with 48. ...., P—R8=Q ch; 49. R×Q, R×R; 50. P—Kt6, R—R1; 51. K—B5, K—R5; 52. P—Kt7, R—K1; 53. K—B6, resigns.

34 Black (Dr. Aitken) to play

White (Golombek)
Munich, 1954

Against the Queen

The chief problem here is how the player with the Queen can win against an opponent with a pawn on the seventh rank about to queen itself, it being understood that the player's King is too far away to help the Queen. The way to win is to chase the King in front of the pawn so that, for one move at any rate, the pawn cannot advance, and to use this tempo

35

to bring up one's own King. In Diagram 35 White wins by 1. Q—R8 ch, K—Kt6; 2. Q—K4 (threatening Q—Kt1); 2. ...., K—R7; 3. Q—R4 ch, K—Kt8 (the first part of our

plan is achieved, now we bring the King up one square);
4. K—B6, K—B8; 5. Q—QB4 ch, K—Q7; 6. Q—Kt3,
K—B8; 7. Q—B3 ch, K—Kt8; 8. K—K5, K—R7; 9. Q—B2,
K—R8; 10. Q—R4 ch, K—Kt8; 11. K—Q4, K—B8 (White
can now proceed to win the pawn by the same process, 12.
Q—B4 ch, K—Q8; 13. Q—Kt3 ch, K—B8; 14. Q—B3 ch,
K—Kt8; 15. K—B4, etc., but there is a slightly quicker way
available); 12. K—B3, P—Kt8=Q (he can put off the loss a
little while by 12. ...., P—Kt8=Kt ch, but his loss would be
quite certain, since the Knight can make no resistance against
a Queen); 13. Q—B4 ch, K—Q8; 14. Q—B1 or Q—Q2,
mate.

There is a similar winning process if the pawn is on the
Q or K or KKt file; *but* place the pawn on the ominous Rook
file and there is a very different story (Diagram 36). White can

36

start off gaily with a check by 1. Q—Kt8 ch, only to find that
Black voluntarily goes in front of the pawn with 1. ....,
K—R8, and the King must be released from its voluntary
prison, otherwise the game is a draw by stalemate.

Just as tragic is the position when the pawn is on the B file
(Diagram 37). At first the process seems to be workable by
1. Q—Kt8 ch, K—R7; 2. Q—B7, K—Kt7; 3. Q—Kt6 ch,
K—R7; 4. Q—B5, K—Kt7; 5. Q—Kt4 ch, K—R7; 6. Q—B3,
K—Kt8; 7. Q—Kt3 ch, and all would be well if Black were to
play 7. ...., K—B8, when we have the normal 8. K—B6,
etc., but, instead, Black replies 7. ...., K—R8! and after
8. Q×P the game is a draw by stalemate.

37

So we have the general rule that the Queen wins against the Knight, the Queen, and King pawn on the seventh rank, but only draws against the Rook or the Bishop pawn. However, there are some exceptions to this rule when the King is near enough to have mating threats. Diagram 38 illustrates this.

38

White allows the pawn to queen and plays 1. K—Kt4, P—B8=Q; 2. K—Kt3, and the mating threat on R2 is not to be averted (apart from giving up the Queen and putting off the mate for a couple of moves).

Minor Piece Endings

The question that is usually asked here is, "Which is better for the end-game, a Knight or a Bishop?" And the answer is that it all depends on the pawn position. If there are many pawns on the board and you have a blocked position then the Knight is the better piece. This also applies when you are left with an ending in which practically all your pawns are on the same colour squares as that occupied by your Bishop, since then that piece has little scope for action. But if a number of pawns have been exchanged, or if it is likely and possible that they will be exchanged, then there will be plenty of open diagonals and the Bishop will be superior to the Knight. It should be pointed out that this is the case in the majority of endings, so that on the whole one might say that the Bishop is the preferable piece. But it pays to keep an open mind on the subject and judge each position according to its own special character.

I give two interesting cases in which the Bishop has clear lines of action and is markedly better than the Knight. First, in Diagram 39 White's Bishop not only controls the long

39   Black (Stahlberg)

White (Najdorf) to play
Zürich, 1953

diagonal, but is so powerful as to give the finishing blow in the game by 55. B—B6 ch, whereupon Black resigns; for if 55. . . . ., K×B; 56. P—B7, and the pawn queens. Or if 55. . . . ., K—Q1; 56. B×P, and now both 56. . . . ., Kt—Q6; 57. P—Kt3, and 56. . . . ., Kt—Q4; 57. P—B7, K—K2; 58. B×P, show how helpless the Knight is in contrast to the active Bishop.

In the next position on Diagram 40 the game was adjourned at this stage, but Black resigned without resuming play. White's winning procedure is to bring the King to Kt7, capture the wretched Knight and then go on to win the KP. Meanwhile, his Bishop controls the two advanced passed pawns and also the long diagonal, whilst the Black King must keep within reach of the distant QRP. Play would go something

like this: 42. ...., P—Kt6; 43. K—Kt5, K—B1; 44. K—R6,
P—B4; 45. P—B3, P×P; 46. P×P, K—B2; 47. K—Kt7,
K—Q3; 48. P—R5, P×P; 49. P×P, K—B2 (if 49. ....,
K×P; 50. P—R6, and the RP queens); 50. K×Kt, K—Q1;
51. K—Kt7, K—B2; 52. K—B7, K—Q3; 53. B—Kt2 and
Black must eventually surrender his KP.

40   Black (Klaman) to play

White (Aronin)
Semi-final, XXIV U.S.S.R. Championship, 1956

How a Knight can triumph over a Bishop is shown in
Diagram 41, where, even though White is a pawn down he has
good winning chances, since the Black pawns get in the way of

41   Black (Filip)

White (Fuchs) to play
Gotha, 1957

the Bishop. Play went 42. P—Kt4, B—Kt3 (a better chance of
saving the game was 42. ...., P—R3, putting another pawn
on a different colour square from the Bishop and thereby giving

it a little more freedom. Even then, White would have had the upper hand after 43. P—R4).

43. Kt—K7 ch, K—B3; 44. Kt—B8, K—K3 (if 44. ....., B—B2; 45. Kt×RP, if 44. ....., B—K6; 45. Kt×QP, in both cases with a won ending for White. Black therefore decides to go in for the pawn ending in which, as will be seen, the opposition plays a great part. The remarkable point is that White has a won end-game, despite being a pawn down).

45. Kt×B, P×Kt; 46. P—R4 (if 46. K×P, P—Kt4; 47. P×P, P—Q4, when White can just attain a draw by 48. K—Kt4), 46. ....., K—B3; 47. K—R5, P—Kt5 (another example of the *zugzwang* mentioned in the chapter on terms; Black must give up a pawn), 48. K×P, K—Kt3; 49. P—R5, P×P; 50. P×P, K—B3; 51. K—R5, K—B2; 52. K—Kt5, K—K3; 53. K—Kt6, K—K2; 54. K—B5, K—Q2 (if 54. ....., K—B2; 55. P—B5, K—K2; 56. P×P ch, K×P; 57. K—B6, and wins); 55. K—B6, K—B2; 56. K—K7, K—B3; 57. K—K6, K—B4 (or 57. ....., K—B2; 58. K—Q5, K—Q2; 59. P—B5, and White wins); 58. K—Q7, K×P; 59. K×P, resigns. (If 59. ....., K—Q5; 60. K—B7, and the White QRP will queen in time to get the winning line as given in the section about Queen against pawn above. Interesting and quite important as this possibility frequently occurs in pawn endings is the line 59. ....., K—Kt4; 60. K×P, K×P; 61. K—Q6, P—Kt4; 62. P—K5, P—Kt5; 63. P—K6, P—Kt6; 64. P—K7, P—Kt7; 65. P—K8 = Q, P—Kt8 = Q; 66. Q—R8 ch, K—Kt5; 67. Q—Kt7 ch, winning the Queen.)

Endings with Bishops of opposite colour are nearly always drawn, as neither side can do each other much damage. This means that if you get into a position where you are a pawn to the bad you should look out for the possibility of bringing about a Bishops of opposite colour ending.

But there are exceptions, these being based as a rule on forcing one or more remote passed pawns. The previous example will have shown that, in endings where pawns are concerned, it is possible to gain space and time by the sacrifice of one or more of the pawns. This comes out even more obviously in the following ending which Black wins even though there are Bishops of opposite colour. This ending is a very clever one, and it made a great impression on me when it was shown to me a month after it had been played by the World Champion, Michael Botvinnik.

42   Black (Botvinnik) to play

White (Kotov)
XXII U.S.S.R. Championship, 1955

Here Black played 59. ...., P—Kt4; 60. BP×P (or 60. RP×P, P—R5; 61. B—Q6, B—B4; 62. P—Kt6, B×P; 63. P—B5, otherwise Black wins by B—B4; 63. ...., B×P; 64. K×P, K—Kt7, and White has to give up his Bishop for the RP); 60. ...., P—Q5 ch!; 61. P×P, K—Kt6; 62. B—R3, K×P; 63. K—Q3, K×P; 64. K—K4, P—R5; 65. K—B3 (if 65. P—Q5, B×P ch, and we have the position in which the Bishop cannot stop one of two distant passed pawns as mentioned earlier in this chapter); 65. ...., B—Q4 ch; White resigns (if 66. K—B2, not 66. ...., P—R6; on account of 67. K—Kt3, but first 66. ...., K—Kt5, when the win is clear).

BISHOP AND PAWN DRAWING POSSIBILITY

Normally a minor piece and a pawn win comfortably against the bare King; but, once we come to the ominous RP the case is different. If then the Bishop is placed on a square of opposite colour to the queening square it is impossible to win. See Diagram 43, where the Black King cannot be winkled out of its corner, and if White places his Bishop on B—B4 and then advances his King to Kt6 the result is stalemate. Naturally, in order to draw, the solitary King must be able to reach the queening square. For, suppose in Diagram 43 the White King were on QKt7 and the Black King on QKt4, then the game is certainly won for White.

43

Bishop and pawn only draw

ROOK AND PAWN ENDINGS

This is the commonest type of ending and, whilst there is an almost infinite variety of Rook and pawn endings, there are also certain basic rules that form a good guide as to how they should be played.

First let us see when a Rook and pawn ending should be drawn and when it should be won. Naturally, these are general rules and there are exceptions, but as a rule the Rook and pawn ending is drawn when the opposing King can get in front of the pawn, and, conversely, the ending is won when the opposing King is cut off from the file on which the pawn stands.

As long ago as 1777 Philidor gave the following example of a drawing position:

44

Black draws by 1. ...., R—QR3; 2. P—K5, R—QKt3; 3. R—R7, R—B3; 4. P—K6, R—B8; 5. K—B6, R—B8

ch, and now the White King cannot escape the checks without leaving the pawn to be captured. The idea for Black in this ending is to keep his Rook on the third rank (so as to prevent the King from coming any nearer), and, once the enemy pawn has reached the sixth rank, to play his Rook to the eighth rank and check the King. For, by placing his pawn on the sixth, White has taken away from his King the possibility of sheltering from the checks behind the pawn.

For the best example of the win we go still further back—to the fifteenth century for the Lucena position, so-called because it appears in the writings of a Spaniard of that period. Now, with the Black King cut off from the file of the pawn, White

45

The Lucena Position

has to solve the problem of a shelter for his King whilst keeping his pawn guarded. This he does by 1. R—B4, R—R8 (or 1. ...., K—K2; 2. R—K4 ch, K—B3; 3. K—B8, and the pawn queens; or 1. ...., R—K7; 2. R—KR4, followed by K—R8); 2. R—K4 ch, K—Q2; 3. K—B7, R—B8 ch; 4. K—Kt6, R—Kt8 ch; 5. K—B6, R—B8 ch (if 5. ...., K—Q3, White drives the King yet another file further away by 6. R—Q4 ch, K—B3, and then forces his pawn to queen by 7. R—Q8, R—B8 ch; 8. K—K5, R—K8 ch; 9. K—B4, R—B8 ch; 10. K—K3, R—K8 ch; 11. K—B2; or if 5. ...., R—Kt7; 6. R—K5, followed by R—KKt5, and the pawn queens); 6. K—Kt5, R—Kt8 ch; 7. R—Kt4, and the pawn queens.

Whilst this winning process can be applied to most positions, there is one main exception. When the pawn is a RP, the ending is usually drawn, as the King can only manœuvre to one side of the pawn.

However, the ending can still be won, providing the enemy King is kept far enough away. This was shown in the following position:

46   Black (Petrosian)

White (Gligoric) to play
Leningrad, 1957

where, in order to win, White must clearly bring his King over to the K side so as to help the pawn to advance. But first he plays 58. R—Kt4! (cutting off the enemy King as far as possible away from the pawn. As a matter of fact, the game would be drawn after 58. K—Q6, K—Kt2; 59. K—K6, K—B2; 60. K—B6, K—Q3; 61. K—Kt5, K—K2; 62. R—B4, R—Kt7 ch, when eventually we shall get the position described in the previous paragraph); 58. ...., K—R3; 59. K—B6, R—B7 ch (urging White to where he wants to go, but if 59. ...., K—R4; 60. R—Kt5 ch, K—R3 or R5; 61. P—R5); 60. K—Q6, R—B8; 61. K—K6, R—B4; 62. K—B6, K—R4; 63. R—KB4, K—Kt3; 64. K—Kt6, R—B8; 65. P—R5, R—Kt8 ch; 66. K—B7, K—B2; 67. R—B6, K—Q2; 68. P—R6, R—KR8; 69. K—Kt7, K—K2; 70. R—KKt6, R—KB8; 71. P—R7, R—B2 ch; 72. K—R6, resigns.

The same rule applies when there is more than one pawn on the board. Consequently, the attacking side must strive to cut off the King from the passed pawn and the defence must do its best to keep the King in front of the dangerous pawn. Thus, in the position in Diagram 47, when Black played 39. ...., K—B4 he was committing a mistake in allowing his King to be cut off from the passed RP. No doubt his idea was

to threaten 40. ...., R—R1 ch; 41. K—Kt3, R×P, with
a clear-cut draw; but White can meet this threat, and correct
was 39. ...., K—R3, keeping the King in front of the passed
pawn. White now won by 40. P—R3, R—R1; 41. K—Kt3,
R—R6 ch; 42. K—R2, R—R1; 43. R—Kt7, R—R5; 44.
K—Kt3, R—R6 ch; 45. K—R4, R—R1; 46. P—Kt4 ch,
K—B5; 47. K—R5, K—Kt6; 48. K—Kt6, R—R3; 49.

47   Black (Wade) to play

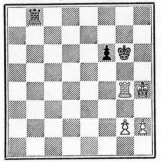

White (Golombek)
Nottingham, 1946

R—KR7, K—B5; 50. R—KB7, K—K4; 51. K—Kt7, R—Kt3;
52. P—R4, K—B5; 53. P—Kt5, P—B4; 54. P—Kt6, K—Kt5;
55. K—R7, K×P; 56. P—Kt7, K—R4 (a last throw); (if now
57. P—Kt8=Q, R—R3 ch; 58. K—Kt7, R—Kt6 ch, and
Black gives up his Rook for the Queen, when the game is
drawn, as White in turn must surrender his Rook for Black's
pawn); 57. R×P ch, K—Kt5; 58. R—B7, resigns.

So far we have been looking at positions where one side was
a pawn up. When the pawns are even the struggle is more
difficult. Here the first rule is to use your King as much as
possible and keep it active. The next is to avoid placing your
Rook in a passive defensive position. It is only by putting it in
an attacking position that you will retain the initiative.
Both these rules are shown working in the position in Diagram
48. It is no use trying to defend the pawn by 72. K—B4, on
account of 72. ...., R—B7 ch, so White places his Rook in
the most attacking position possible by 72. R—Q7, R×P (if
72. ...., K—B1; 73. P—B6, K—K1; 74. R—K7 ch, K—B1;
75. R—Kt7, K—K1; 76. R—Kt8 ch, K—Q2; 77. R—KB8,

K—K3; 78. R—K8 ch, K—B4; 79. P—K6, and the BP queens); 73. K—B4, R—Kt8; 74. P—K6, R—B8 ch; 75. K—K5 R—K8 ch; 76. K—Q6, P—R4; 77. R×P ch, K—Kt1; 78. K—K7, resigns. (Because of 78. ...., P—R5; 79. K—B6, P—R6; 80. R—Kt7 ch, K—R1; 81. R—Kt3, etc.)

48   Black (Euwe)

White (Gligoric) to play
Zürich, 1953

In the next position (Diagram 49) we again see the power of the active King; but another important point emerges. In order to get the most advantage out of the possession of a

49   Black (Stahlberg)

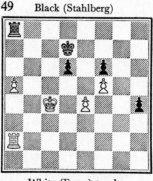

White (Euwe) to play
Zürich, 1953

passed pawn, the Rook should be placed behind it so as to help its advance. The game continued: 49. P—R6, K—B3; 50. P—R7, P—R6 (if 50. ...., K—Kt2; 51. K—Q5, R×P; 52. R—R2, R—R4 ch; 53. K×P, R—R4; 54. R×P, followed

by R—R6 with a won ending); 51. K—Q4, K—B2 (if 51. ....,
P—R7; first 52. R—B2 ch, and if then 52. ...., K—Q2;
53. R×P, or if 52. ...., K—Kt3; 53. R×P, R×P; 54. K—Q5,
and wins); 52. K—Q5, K—Q2; 53. R—R3, P—R7; 54.
R—R1!, R—K1 (remarkably enough, Black was now in
zugzwang. If (*a*) 54. ...., P—R8=Q; 55. R×Q, R×P;
56. R—R7 ch, winning the Rook; or (*b*) 54. ...., K—Q1;
55. K×P, R×P; 56. R×R, P—R8=Q; 57. R—R8 mate;
(*c*) 54. ...., K—B1; 55. K—B6, K—Q1; 56. K×P, as in line
(*b*); (*d*) 54. ...., K—K2; 55. K—B6, R—R1; 56. K—Kt7;
(*e*) 54. ...., K—B2; 55. K—K6, K—Kt3; 56. R—R1, R×P;
57. R×P, and wins; or, finally, (*f*) 54. ...., R—R1; 55.
R—R1, K—K2; 56. R×P); 55. R—R1, R—K4 ch; 56.
K—Q4, R—R4; 57. R×P, K—B3; 58. R—R7, R—R5 ch;
59. K—K3, R—R6 ch; 60. K—B4, R—R8; 61. R—KB7,
K—B4; 62. R×P, R×P; 63. R—K6, R—R8; 64. P—B6,
K—B3; 65. K—B5, K—Q2; 66. R—K7 ch, K—Q1; 67.
K—K6, resigns.

QUEEN ENDINGS

Though you will meet these less often than Rook endings,
they still represent an important phase in the endings and are
amongst the most difficult of all to handle accurately. But
once this is achieved I must say that there is nothing quite so
satisfying in chess.

Before coming to Queen and pawn endings, we should first
have a look to see how the Queen fares against other pieces.
Against a minor piece it has no difficulty whatsoever in winning; nor does it usually have much trouble in dealing with
two minor pieces. When we come to the Rook, it is, however,
quite a different story. The Queen is roughly equivalent to
two Rooks, but in the ending you will usually find, providing
both Kings are in reasonable safety, that it is preferable to
have the two Rooks. The reason for this is that these two
pieces in co-operation can often capture pawns whilst the
Queen must look on helplessly without being able to recapture.

Even against one Rook the Queen experiences difficulties in
winning and the process is quite an elaborate one.

THE QUEEN VERSUS THE ROOK

When the King and the Rook are far apart, the winning process is usually quite simple, and consists of a series of checks, at the end of which the Queen wins the Rook. It is when the King and Rook are near each other that the difficulty exists. However, the idea to follow is to force the enemy King to the back rank and then compel the Rook to leave the King or else by a combined series of moves with King and Queen to construct a mating net. An example of this is shown in Diagram 50:

50

White wins by 1. Q—B6 ch, K—K1; 2. Q—R8 ch (not 2. K—K6, R—Q3 ch; 3. K × R, stalemate); 2. ...., K—B2; 3. Q—R7 ch, K—K1; 4. Q—Kt8 ch, K—K2; 5. Q—B8!, R—Q7 (White's last subtle move forced the Rook away from the King; for if 5. ...., R—Q1; 6. Q—K6 ch, K—B1; 7. K—B6, and Black is mated); 6. Q—B5 ch, K—Q2; 7. Q—Kt5 ch, K—B1; 8. K—K6, R—QB7; 9. K—K7, R—B2 ch; 10. K—Q6, R—QR2 (there are two alternatives here: (1) 10. ...., R—B8; 11. Q—R4, K—Kt1; 12. Q—Kt3 ch, K—B1; 13. Q—R3, R—Q8 ch; 14. K—B6, and now Black is mated or else has to give up the Rook; (2) 10. ...., R—KKt2; 11. Q—KB5 ch, K—Kt2; 12. Q—B3 ch, K—R2; 13. Q—B2 ch, K—R3; 14. Q—R2 ch, K—Kt2 or elsewhere; 15. Q—Kt2 ch, picking up the Rook); 11. Q—K8 ch, K—Kt2; 12. Q—Q7 ch, K—Kt1; 13. Q—Q8 ch, K—Kt2; 14. Q—B7 ch, K—R3; Q—B6 ch, K—R4; 16. K—B5, and mate or loss of the Rook is inevitable.

There are also some positions in which, owing to the stalemate possibilities that so often arise in connection with the Queen, Black can even force a draw. Such a position is shown in Diagram 51 where Black draws by 1. ...., R—R2 ch;

51

2. K—Kt2, R—Kt2 ch; 3. K—B3, R—B2 ch; 4. K—Kt4 (White cannot escape with his King to the K file by 4. K—K4, on account of 4. ...., R—K2); 4. ...., R—Kt2 ch; 5. K—B5, R—B2 ch; 6. K—Kt6, R—Kt2 ch; 7. K—R6 (if 7. K—B6, R—Kt3 ch; 8. K×R, stalemate); 7. ...., R—R2 ch!; 8. K—Kt6, R—R3 ch!; 9. K×R, stalemate.

QUEEN AND PAWN ENDINGS

Apart from the level ones that should end in a draw, there are two main types: that in which one side possesses a passed pawn or a potential passed pawn and that in which one side enjoys an enduring attack on a weakened King position.

In the first case it is the player who has a remote passed pawn that usually has the upper hand. For an example see Diagram 52, where, although White is a pawn up, the dangerous QRP wins for Black as follows: 42. ...., Q—K2 ch; 43. K—B4, P—R6; 44. K—K3, Q—Kt2; 45. Q—Q8 ch, K—R2; 46. Q—R5, Q—Kt7; 47. Q—B7, Q—Kt6; 48. P—Kt4, P—R7; 49. Q—R5, Q—Kt7; 50. Q—B7, K—Kt1; 51. Q—Q8 ch, K—Kt2; 52. Q—Q4 ch, K—R2; 53. Q—B4, Q—Kt3 ch; 54. K—K2, Q—R2; 55. P×P, P—R8=Q; 56. P×P ch, P×P; White resigns.

52 Black (Cholmov) to play

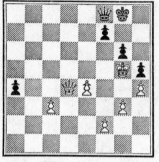

White (Bannik)
XXIII U.S.S.R. Championship, 1956

The other type is shown in Diagram 53 where, though Black is a passed pawn to the good, he cannot win simply by advancing it, since this gives White good drawing chances (after, say, 42. ...., P—Q5; 43. Q—R8 ch, K—Kt2; 44. Q—Q8, etc.), so he plays 42. ...., Q—K8 ch; 43. K—Kt2, Q—K5 ch; 44. K—R3, Q—B4 ch; 45. K—Kt2, Q—B7 ch;

53 Black (Fuster) to play

White (Watzl)
Match, Austria-Hungary, 1947

46. K—R3, P—Kt4 (the fact that White's K side has been weakened earlier in the game now comes home to roost); 47. Q—B1, Q—B4 ch; 48. K—Kt2, P×P; 49. P×P, Q—Kt5 ch; 50. K—R1, P—R4; 51. Q—B2, P—R5; 52. Q—B1, P—R6, and White resigns, since his only way of preventing mate is by exchanging Queens with 53. Q—KKt1, when Black has a simple won pawn ending.

Finally, here is an example of a Queen and pawn ending that should not have been won (Diagram 54); and, in case you have become a little depressed at the difficulties involved and feel that only grandmasters should be allowed to play Queen and pawn endings, let me point out that it was a grandmaster who made the mistake here. White has been checking the King up and down, and so far the Black King has found no safe haven. In fact, White could still play 57. Q—QB1 ch, and if 57. ...., K—K4; 58. Q—B5 ch, when the game is a certain

54   Black (Keres)

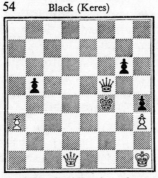

White (Stahlberg) to play
Zürich, 1953

draw, as the Black King cannot reach the side, where its only possible refuge lies.

Instead of doing this, White played 57. Q—Q2 ch?, K—K4; 58. Q—B3 ch, K—Q4; 59. Q—Kt3 ch, K—B3; 60. Q—QB3 ch, K—Kt2; 61. Q—Kt7 ch, K—R3 (the checks are over and it is Black's turn to harry the King); 62. Q—B3, Q—B8 ch; 63. K—R2, Q—B7 ch; 64. K—R1, K—Kt3; 65. Q—B8, Q—K8 ch; 66. K—Kt2, Q—K5 ch; 67. K—Kt1, Q—Q5 ch; White resigns because of 68. K—Kt2, Q—Q4 ch; 69. K—R2, Q—Q3 ch; 70. K—Kt2 or R1, Q—B3 ch; or 70. K—Kt1, Q—B4 ch, in any case forcing the exchange of Queens and a won pawn ending.

CHAPTER IV

THE OPENINGS

THERE are three main points to be observed when starting a game of chess: (1) development; (2) correct placing of pieces; and (3) control of the centre.

The number of the various openings is almost legion, and you could hardly be blamed at feeling bewildered when wandering in the maze that is usually provided by text-books on the openings. To complicate matters, quite a number have double-barrelled and outlandish names that make them look more fiendish than they really are—Van Hennig-Schara Gambit, Hamppe-Allgaier and Boden-Kieseritsky Gambits—all these give one a fright before they are seen in action on the board.

But, as long as the three main points above are borne in mind, you should not go far wrong in the openings. For the openings are only good in so far as they obey the basic rules of development.

Point No. 1 is concerned with the bringing out of your pieces. It stands to reason that you are not going to get very far with the game if you fail to bring your pieces out, and that quickly. So refrain from too many pawn moves in the early stages of the game. On the whole, for your very earliest moves you should only move the pawns so as to allow your pieces to come out.

Point No. 2 should be taken in relation to point No. 1. It is of no use bringing out your pieces so as to place them in positions where they are exerting no influence on the course of the game. Here the general rule is to avoid placing them on the edges of the board; most pieces lose much of their effectiveness when posted on the Rook files, and this applies in particular to the Knights, whose usefulness is directly halved when stationed on a Rook file.

Point No. 2 also contains a most important rule. As far as possible, see that your pieces are working together. You will be surprised to see how much greater the strength of your pieces is when they co-operate with each other than when they are working singly. Two Rooks working together on the same file or rank form a battering ram of enormous power; two Bishops on adjacent diagonals have a razor-sharp cutting power, and so on all along the line from King to pawns.

Point No. 3 has a bearing on points 1 and 2. If you control the centre then you can develop your pieces more quickly and can post them in the most favourable positions. Then too the centre is at once a sort of cross-roads and a power-house from which you can launch an attack. Without command of the centre you have very little chance of being successful in either a King- or a Queen-side attack.

This question of the centre provides you with a method of judging which openings are really worth-while. All openings have something to do with centre control, and it is those openings that have most to do with it and those openings that are most successful in gaining this control that must be regarded as the best.

I propose in this chapter to deal more fully with some important openings that obey the rules set out above and to touch more lightly on most of the other openings. I should perhaps emphasise that it is of little use learning off these openings parrot-fashion and playing moves just because I, or anyone else, from Alekhine and Capablanca downwards, have recommended them. What is vitally important is that you should understand what the moves are for, what each opening is striving to achieve and what is the ordered plan behind the strings of variations.

I start with an old-fashioned opening that still retains quite a kick.

THE GIUOCO PIANO

These two Italian words mean "gentle or slow game", and the opening derives its name from the fact that it seemed to the Italians to be a much milder way of starting the game than by playing a gambit. All the same, as will be seen, it contains its own quota of violence.

1. P—K4

One of the best first moves on the board—though not the best, since there is no such thing as a best first move. All that can be said is that there are a number of good first moves, of which this is an outstanding example. It already stakes some claim on the centre and helps to develop both the Queen and the King Bishops.

1. ....   P—K4

The same remark applies to this move for Black as in the note above.

2. Kt—KB3

On the whole, it is preferable to bring out the Knight before the Bishop, as it is a slow-stepping piece. Remember, too, it works better near the centre than on the edge of the board. In any case, here we develop it and at once attack a pawn.

2. ....   Kt—QB3
3. B—B4

With this move one of the ideas in the Giuoco becomes clear: attack on Black's weak KB2, an attack which can eventually be reinforced by such moves as Q—Kt3 and Kt—KKt5.

3. ....   B—B4

Black can also play 3. ...., Kt—B3 (the Two Knights' Defence; see p. 64).

4. P—B3

This is the move which gives the Giuoco the right to be considered an opening worth playing, since it prepares an onslaught on the centre by P—Q4. Also note that at some future stage White will be able to bring his Queen to Kt3 with effect.

White has quite a number of alternatives here. He may play 4. P—QKt4 (the Evans' Gambit; see p. 61) or 4. o—o (the Max Lange; see p. 63); or, finally, the quiet 4. P—Q3, P—Q3; 5. Kt—B3, Kt—B3; 6. B—KKt5, a line known as the Canal variation, after the Peruvian master who had some success with it in the international tournament at Carlsbad, 1929. Black should not have much trouble against this line, e.g. 6. ...., P—KR3; 7. B×Kt, Q×B; 8. Kt—Q5, Q—Q1; 9. P—B3, P—QR3; 10. P—QKt4, B—R2; 11. P—QR4, B—K3; 12. Q—Kt3, o—o; 13. Kt—K3, Q—Q2.

4. .... Kt—B3

Black replies with a move that continues his development and also counter-attacks on White's KP.

Quite a different system of defence arises out of 4. ...., Q—K2; by which Black concentrates on maintaining the central point, K4. The game can then go 5. P—Q4, B—Kt3; 6. o—o, P—Q3; 7. P—KR3, Kt—B3; 8. R—K1, o—o; 9. Kt—R3, K—R1; 10. Kt—B2, Kt—Q1; 11. P—QKt3, B—K3; 12. B—B1, Kt—Kt1; 13. Kt—K3, P—KB3; 14. Kt—Q5, Q—B2; 15. P—B4, and White has the advantage.

5. P—Q4   P×P
6. P×P   B—Kt5 ch
7. Kt—B3

A move that leads to some very exciting variations. The obvious alternative is 7. B—Q2, but then Black can gain easy equality with 7. ...., B×B ch; 8. QKt×B, P—Q4; 9. P×P, KKt×P; 10. Q—Kt3, Kt(B3)—K2; 11. o—o, o—o; 12. KR—K1, P—QB3; 13. P—QR4, Q—B2; 14. QR—B1, Q—B5; 15. Kt—K4, B—B4; 16. Kt—B5, P—QKt3; 17. Kt—Q3, B×Kt; 18. B×B, QR—Q1.

Another interesting possibility is 7. K—B1, when, however, Black frees himself by 7. ...., P—Q4!; 8. P×P, KKt×P; 9. Kt—B3, B—K3; 10. Q—K2, o—o;

7. ....   Kt×KP
8. o—o

A gallant move, leaving Black to choose between two ways of capturing White's QKt.

55

Variation One

8. ....   B×Kt
9. P—Q5

Again a lively move to keep the tension high. After 9. P×B, P—Q4, Black would stand very well indeed.

9. ....   B—B3

Best; if 9. ...., o—o; 10. P×B, Kt—K2; 11. R—K1, Kt—KB3; 12. P—Q6, P×P; 13. B—R3, with great advantage to White. Or if 9. ...., B—R4; 10. P×Kt, QP×P; 11. Q—R4, B—Kt3; 12. B×P ch, K×B; 13. Q×Kt, Q—Q4; 14. Kt—Kt5 ch, with a very strong attack for White.

10. R—K1   Kt—K2
11. R×Kt   P—Q3
12. B—Kt5   B×B
13. Kt×B   o—o

This allows White to sacrifice on KR7 with some very intriguing possibilities. The alternative is 13. ...., P—KR3, but White then gains a fierce attack by 14. B—Kt5 ch, B—Q2; 15. Q—K2, K—B1; 16. QR—K1.

14. Kt×RP   K×Kt

Also possible is 14. ...., B—B4; 15. R—R4, R—K1; 16. Kt—Kt5, when White still has a strong attack.

15. Q—R5 ch   K—Kt1
16. R—R4   P—KB4

Who has the better of it here? Well, it is clear that White can force a draw by perpetual check if he likes with 17. Q—R7 ch, K—B2; 18. R—R6, R—KKt1; 19. R—K1, Q—B1; 20. B—Kt5, R—R1; 21. Q×R, P×R; 22. Q—R7 ch, K—B3; 23. R×Kt, Q×R; 24. Q×RP ch, etc. but whether he has anything more than this is dubious.

Variation Two (*see Diagram 55*)

8. ....   Kt×Kt

A more risky line for Black than the previous one.

9. P×Kt   P—Q4

If 9. ...., B×P; 10. B—R3, Kt—K2; 11. Q—Kt3, P—Q4; 12. Q×B, P×B; 13. KR—K1, B—K3; 14. B×Kt, K×B; 15. P—Q5, Q×P; 16. QR—Q1, with an irresistible attack for White.

10. P×B   P×B
11. R—K1 ch   Kt—K2
12. B—Kt5

Stronger than 12. Q—K2, B—K3, when 13. B—Kt5 can be met by 13. ...., Q—Q4.

12. ....   P—KB3

He cannot now play 12. ...., B—K3; on account of 13. B×Kt, followed by 14. P—Q5, winning a piece whichever way Black recaptures.

13. Q—K2   B—Kt5

If 13. ...., P×B; 14. Q×P, P—B3; 15. R—K5, and White has a winning attack.

14. B—B4   K—B2
15. Q×P ch   Kt—Q4
16. Kt—Q2   B—K3
17. B—Kt3   P—B3
18. Kt—K4

and White, who will establish his Kt on QB5, has the better game.

THE RUY LOPEZ

This powerful opening has always enjoyed a steady popularity and to-day it is the most frequently employed of all K-side openings. No opening gives White such an enduring pressure on Black's K4 as the Ruy and few afford White so many attacking chances both on the Q and K side.

It is, however, a difficult opening to play either as White or Black, not only because in the course of its long history it has acquired myriads of variations, but also because of the mixture of the ideas involved. At one moment you have to think of combining furiously, of sacrificing pawns and pieces to open up the game for an attack and of striving with all your might and main for an attack against the enemy King; at another you have to concern yourself with positional considerations, to study the nature of the pawn structure, the possibility of gaining a favourable end-game and the investment of weak squares or the buttressing of strong points.

Still—or perhaps I should rather say all the more—it is emphatically an opening that repays study and practice. Master the Ruy Lopez and you are well on the way to mastery at chess.

The main defence to this opening is named after the great nineteenth-century American master, Paul Morphy.

THE MORPHY DEFENCE

1. P—K4   P—K4
2. Kt—KB3   Kt—QB3
3. B—Kt5   P—QR3

Too passive in nature is the Steinitz Defence, 3. ....., P—Q3, since White gains command of greater space by 4. P—Q4, B—Q2; 5. Kt—B3, P×P; 6. Kt×P, Kt—B3; 7. o—o, B—K2; 8. B×Kt, P×B; 9. P—QKt3, o—o; 10. B—Kt2, R—K1; 11. Q—B3, B—KB1; 12. P—KR3, P—Kt3; 13. QR—Q1.

4. B—R4

Taking off the Knight with the idea of winning the KP does not work yet, because of 4. B×Kt, QP×B; 5. Kt×P, Q—Q5. However, this exchange variation can be played as follows: 4. B×Kt, QP×B; 5. Kt—B3, P—B3; 6. P—Q4, P×P; 7. Q×P, Q×Q; 8. Kt×Q, B—Q2; 9. B—K3, o—o—o, with about an equal game, though I rather prefer Black's, since his two Bishops will prove powerful.

4. ....   Kt—B3

Another defence often used is 4. ....., P—Q3 (the Steinitz Defence Deferred), to which White replies 5. P—B3, B—Q2; 6. P—Q4, Kt—B3; 7. o—o, B—K2; 8. R—K1, o—o; 9. QKt—Q2, with rather the better chances.

5. o—o

White can leave his KP unprotected, since Black, by capturing the pawn, will open up the position in the centre. This in turn means that White, at the very least, will be able to regain his pawn without disadvantage.

5. ....   B—K2

This leads to the close variation of the Morphy Defence, so called because the centre is not opened up in the early stages of the game, at any rate.

The open line commences with 5. ...., Kt×P, and a variation that has been popular of recent years runs 6. P—Q4, P—QKt4; 7. B—Kt3, P—Q4; 8. P×P, B—K3; 9. Q—K2 (White plans to get pressure on the Q file by R—Q1—always try to get a Rook opposite your opponent's Queen at any stage in the game); 9. ...., B—K2; 10. R—Q1, o—o; 11. P—B4, KtP×P; 12. B×P, B—QB4; 13. B—K3, B×B; 14. Q×B, Q—Kt1; 15. B—Kt3, Kt—R4; 16. QKt—Q2, when White has rather the better game.

6. R—K1

Another way of protecting the KP is by 6. Q—K2, with an idea similar to that given in the previous note—to get the Rook opposite the Queen. Against this idea Black's best plan is to get his Queen to QB2 as follows 6. ...., P—QKt4; 7. B—Kt3, P—Q3; 8. P—B3, Kt—QR4; 9. B—B2, P—B4; 10. P—Q4, Q—B2; 11. R—Q1, o—o; 12. B—Kt5, B—Kt5; 13. P×KP, P×P; 14. QKt—Q2, KR—Q1; 15. Kt—B1, Kt—R4; 16. P—KR3, B×Kt; 17. Q×B, B×B; 18. Q×Kt, Q—K2, with equality.

6. ....   P—QKt4

Now that White was threatening to win the KP by B×Kt, followed by Kt×P, Black must drive the Bishop away.

7. B—Kt3   P—Q3

Black may also go in for counter-attack here, at the cost of a pawn by 7. ...., o—o; 8. P—B3, P—Q4 (the Marshall Variation); but White can safely retain his pawn by 9. P×P, Kt×P; 10. Kt×P, Kt×Kt; 11. R×Kt, Kt—B3; 12. P—Q4, B—Q3; 13. R—K2, B—Kt2; 14. Kt—Q2, Q—Q2; 15. Kt—B1.

8. P—B3

Preparing to attack the centre by P—Q4 whilst giving the Bishop a further retreat if attacked by Black's QKt.

8. ....   o—o
9. P—KR3

So as to prevent Black from usefully developing his QB (after 9. P—Q4, B—Kt5).

9. ....   Kt—QR4

Black's idea is to attack on the Q side, and at the same time he plans to maintain his pawn on K4 so as to have some hold on the centre, as will be seen.

10. B—B2   P—B4
11. P—Q4   Q—B2
12. QKt—Q2

This is the standard position in the Ruy Lopez which has occurred countless times in tournament and club play. White's aim will be to create an attack on the K side, whilst Black will counter-attack on the other wing. For White the manœuvre Kt—KB1 and then either to K3 or Kt3 with the further aims of Q5 and B5 often recurs; for Black the grouping of his Rooks on QB1 and Q1, together with such pawn advances as P—QKt5 and P—QB5, are equally familiar; whilst both sides will do their best to obtain control of the Q file.

56

No less than seven main lines can arise from this position, and I give a sample of each:

(1) 12. ...., Kt—B3; 13. P—Q5, Kt—Q1; 14. P—QR4, R—Kt1; 15. P—B4, B—Q2; 16. Kt—B1, Kt—K1; 17. P—KKt4, and White will continue the attack by Kt—Kt3, K—R2 and R—KKt1.

(2) 12. ...., Kt—Q2; 13. Kt—B1, Kt—Kt3; 14. Kt—K3, P—B3; 15. P—QKt3, Kt—B3; 16. P—Q5, Kt—Q1, and White will follow a similar method of attack to that given in variation 1.

(3) 12. ...., B—Kt2; 13. P—QR4, BP×P; 14. BP×P, P—Kt5; 15. P—QKt3, QR—B1; 16. B—Kt1, P—Q4; 17. QP×P, Kt×KP; 18. Kt×Kt, P×Kt; 19. B×P, KR—Q1; 20. B—Q2, B×B; 21. R×B, Q—Kt2, and Black has some pressure in return for the pawn sacrificed.

(4) 12. ...., B—Q2; 13. Kt—B1, Kt—B5; 14. Kt—K3, Kt×Kt; 15. B×Kt, B—B3; 16. Kt—Q2, with a good game for White.

(5) 12. ...., R—K1; 13. Kt—B1, B—Kt2; 14. P—Q5, B—QB1; 15. Kt—K3, B—B1; 16. K—R1, P—Kt3; 17. P—KKt4, B—KKt2; 18. R—KKt1, and White has a good K-side attack.

(6) 12. ...., R—Q1; 13. Kt—B1, BP×P; 14. P×P, P—Q4; 15. Kt×P, P×P; 16. Kt—Kt3, B—Q3; 17. Q—K2, B×Kt; 18. P×B, Q×P; 19. B—Q2, and White, who will play B—B3 next move, has the advantage.

(7) 12. ...., BP×P (perhaps the most popular variation nowadays); 13. P×P, Kt—B3; 14. Kt—Kt3, P—QR4; 15. B—K3, P—R5; 16. Kt(Kt3)—Q2, Kt—QKt5; 17. B—Kt1, P—R6; 18. Q—Kt3, Q—R4; 19. QP×P, QP×P; 20. Q×P, Q×Q; 21. P×Q, R×P; 22. Kt×P, B—K3; 23. Kt(K5)—B3, Kt×RP; 24. Kt—Q4, Kt—B6; 25. R×R, B×R; 26. Kt×B, P×Kt; 27. B—B2, and White's game is to be preferred (two Bishops!).

This will have given you a general picture of Morphy's Defence; but other defences crop up from time to time and here are specimens of the most interesting ones:

THE BERLIN DEFENCE

1. P—K4, P—K4; 2. Kt—KB3, Kt—QB3; 3. B—Kt5, Kt—B3; 4. o—o, Kt×P; 5. P—Q4, B—K2; 6. Q—K2,

Kt—Q3; 7. B×Kt, KtP×B; 8. P×P, Kt—Kt2; 9. Kt—B3, o—o; 10. Kt—Q4, B—B4; 11. R—Q1, B×Kt; 12. R×B, R—K1; 13. Q—R5, P—Kt3; 14. Q—B3, R×P; 15. B—B4, R—K1; 16. QR—Q1, and although he is a pawn down, White has the better game, owing to the strong pressure he exerts on the position.

BIRD'S DEFENCE

1. P—K4, P—K4; 2. Kt—KB3, Kt—QB3; 3. B—Kt5, Kt—Q5 (an eccentric defence that cannot be good, since it loses time); 4. Kt×Kt, P×Kt; 5. o—o, P—QB3; 6. B—B4, Kt—B3; 7. R—K1, P—Q3; 8. P—QB3, Q—Kt3; 9. Q—Kt3, Q×Q; 10. B×Q, P×P; 11. KtP×P, B—K2; 12. B—R3, and White, with the threat of P—K5, has the better game.

THE CLASSICAL DEFENCE

1. P—K4, P—K4; 2. Kt—KB3, Kt—QB3; 3. B—Kt5, B—B4; 4. P—B3, Kt—B3; 5. P—Q4, P×P; 6. P—K5, Kt—K5; 7. o—o, P—Q4; 8. P×P e.p., o—o; 9. P×BP, Q×P; 10. P×P, B—Q3; 11. Kt—B3, Kt×Kt; 12. P×Kt, B—KKt5; 13. P—KR3, and White is a safe pawn to the good, with little to fear in the way of counter-attack.

SCHLIEMANN DEFENCE

1. P—K4, P—K4; 2. Kt—KB3, Kt—QB3; 3. B—Kt5, P—B4 (a violent attempt to seize the initiative that should recoil on Black's own head); 4. Kt—B3, P×P; 5. QKt×P, P—Q4; 6. Kt×P, P×Kt; 7. Kt×Kt, Q—Q4; 8. P—QB4, Q—Q3; 9. Kt×P dis. ch, K—Q1; 10. Kt×B, K×Kt; 11. P—Q4, P×P e.p.; 12. o—o, with much the better game for White.

There are about another twenty King-side openings which you are likely to meet from time to time, though none of them have anywhere near the popularity of the Ruy Lopez. I give a main variation of each of the more important, with a word or two about the idea of the opening.

Bishop's Opening

White tries to attack Black's KB2, generally reckoned his weakest point; but the attack is a bit too obvious and Black should have no difficulty in repelling it.

1. P—K4, P—K4; 2. B—B4, Kt—KB3; 3. P—Q3, P—B3; 4. P—B4, P×P; 5. B×P, P—Q4; 6. P×P, Kt×P; 7. Q—B3, B—K3; 8. Kt—K2, Kt×B; 9. Q×Kt, B×B; 10. Q×B, B—Q3 and Black has an excellent game.

Centre Game

An opening certainly not to be recommended for White, since he brings his Queen out too early in the game and loses time with it in retreating from the attack of enemy minor pieces.

1. P—K4, P—K4; 2. P—Q4, P×P; 3. Q×P, Kt—QB3; 4. Q—K3, Kt—B3; 5. Kt—QB3, B—K2; 6. B—Q2, P—Q4; 7. P×P, Kt×P; 8. Kt×Kt, Q×Kt; 9. Kt—K2, o—o; 10. Kt—B3, Q—QB4, and the game is level.

Danish Gambit

A more interesting off-shoot of the previous opening but one which also yields Black a good game.

1. P—K4, P—K4; 2. P—Q4, P×P; 3. P—QB3, P×P; 4. B—QB4, P×P; 5. B×P, P—Q4; 6. B×P, Kt—KB3; 7. B×P ch, K×B; 8. Q×Q, B—Kt5 ch; 9. Q—Q2, B×Q ch; 10. Kt×B, P—B4; 11. P—B4, Kt—B3, and Black has the advantage.

Evans' Gambit

An attractive opening in which White sacrifices a pawn to gain development and open lines for his pieces. It arises out of the Giuoco Piano.

1. P—K4, P—K4; 2. Kt—KB3, Kt—QB3; 3. B—B4, B—B4; 4. P—QKt4, B×P; 5. P—B3, B—R4; 6. P—Q4, P—Q3; 7. B—KKt5, P—B3; 8. Q—Kt3, P×B; 9. B×Kt, Q—B3; 10. P×P, P×P; 11. o—o, and White's attack is worth the pawn sacrificed.

Four Knights' Game

A very steady opening with which one can hardly lose as White, but this is hardly the kind of aim one should have as the first player.

1. P—K4, P—K4; 2. Kt—KB3, Kt—QB3; 3. Kt—B3, Kt—B3; 4. B—Kt5, B—Kt5; 5. o—o, o—o; 6. P—Q3, B×Kt;

7. P×B, P—Q3; 8. B—Kt5, Q—K2; 9. R—K1, Kt—Q1; 10. P—Q4, Kt—K3; 11. B—QB1, P—B4; 12. B—B1, BP×P; 13. P×P, Q—B2, and the game is level.

Greco Counter-Gambit

Black makes a violent attempt, which should not succeed, to wrest the initiative from White.

1. P—K4, P—K4; 2. Kt—KB3, P—KB4; 3. Kt×P, Q—B3; 4. Kt—B4, P×P; 5. Kt—B3, Q—KKt3; 6. P—Q3, B—Kt5; 7. B—Q2, B×Kt; 8. B×B, Kt—KB3; 9. P×P, Kt×P; 10. B—Q3, and White has the advantage, since after 10. ...., Q×P; 11. Q—R5 ch gives him a won game, and therefore Black has nothing better than 10. ...., o—o; 11. o—o.

King's Bishop Gambit

A lively opening in which White again tries to assault Black's KB2, but with more force than in the Bishop's Opening.

1. P—K4, P—K4; 2. P—KB4, P×P; 3. B—B4, Kt—KB3; 4. Kt—QB3, P—B3; 5. Q—B3, P—Q4; 6. P×P, B—Q3; 7. P—Q3, B—KKt5; 8. Q—B2, o—o; 9. KKt—K2, R—K1; 10. o—o, P×P, with a good game for Black.

King's Knight Gambit

Better than the Bishop's Gambit, though only to the extent of securing equality.

1. P—K4, P—K4; 2. P—KB4, P×P; 3. Kt—KB3, P—KKt4; 4. P—KR4, P—Kt5; 5. Kt—K5, Kt—KB3; 6. P—Q4, P—Q3; 7. Kt—Q3, Kt×P; 8. B×P, Q—K2; 9. Q—K2, B—Kt2; 10. P—B3, B—B4; 11. Kt—Q2, Kt×Kt; 12. K×Kt, Q×Q ch; 13. B×Q, Kt—Q2, with a level game.

Falkbeer Counter-Gambit

This is an excellent method of replying to the King's Gambit.

1. P—K4, P—K4; 2. P—KB4, P—Q4; 3. KP×P, P—K5; 4. P—Q3, Kt—KB3; 5. Kt—Q2, P×P; 6. B×P, Q×P; 7. KKt—B3, B—KKt5; 8. P—KR3, B×Kt; 9. Kt×B, B—K2; 10. o—o, o—o, with an equal game.

MAX LANGE

Another attack that can arise out of the Giuoco Piano and a very fierce one—whilst it lasts.

1. P—K4, P—K4; 2. Kt—KB3, Kt—QB3; 3. B—B4, B—B4; 4. o—o, Kt—B3; 5. P—Q4, P×P; 6. P—K5, P—Q4; 7. P×Kt, P×B; 8. R—K1 ch, B—K3; 9. Kt—Kt5, Q—Q4; 10. Kt—QB3, Q—B4; 11. Kt(B3)—K4, o—o—o; 12. Kt×B, P×Kt; 13. P—KKt4, Q—K4; 14. P×P, KR—Kt1; 15. B—R6, P—Q6; P—B3, P—Q7; 17. R—K2, R—Q6; and Black has the upper hand.

PETROFF DEFENCE

Black defends by counter-attack and attains a rough equality.

1. P—K4, P—K4; 2. Kt—KB3, Kt—KB3; 3. Kt×P, P—Q3; 4. Kt—KB3, Kt×P; 5. P—Q4, P—Q4; 6. B—Q3, B—K2; 7. o—o; Kt—QB3; 8. R—K1, B—KKt5; 9. P—B4, Kt—B3; 10. P×P, KKt×P; 11. Kt—B3, o—o; 12. B—K4, B—K3, the game is level.

PHILIDOR DEFENCE

Black adopts a passive defensive system and as a result gets cramped for space.

1. P—K4, P—K4; 2. Kt—KB3, P—Q3; 3. P—Q4, Kt—Q2; 4. B—QB4, P—QB3; 5. Kt—B3, B—K2; 6. o—o, P—KR3; 7. P—QR4, KKt—B3; 8. P—QKt3, Q—B2; 9. B—Kt2, o—o; 10. Q—Q2, with advantage to White.

PONZIANI OPENING

An attempt to gain control of the centre that Black can easily refute by vigorous play.

1. P—K4, P—K4; 2. Kt—KB3, Kt—QB3; 3. P—B3, P—Q4; 4. Q—R4, Kt—B3; 5. Kt×P, B—Q3; 6. Kt×Kt, P×Kt; 7. Q×P ch, B—Q2; 8. Q—R6, P×P; 9. B—Kt5, o—o; 10. B×B, Q×B, and Black's superior development more than compensates him for the pawn minus.

SCOTCH GAME

A simple line that opens up the centre too early to hope to retain the initiative. A little more preparation is necessary.

1. P—K4, P—K4; 2. Kt—KB3, Kt—QB3; 3. P—Q4, P×P; 4. Kt×P, B—B4; 5. B—K3, Q—B3; 6. P—QB3, KKt—K2; 7. Kt—B2, B×B; 8. Kt×B, Q—K4; 9. Q—B3, o—o; 10. B—B4, P—Q3; 11. Kt—Q2, B—K3, with complete equality.

SCOTCH GAMBIT

White offers up a pawn in the interests of development, but Black can easily equalise as long as he does not cling on to his extra pawn too obstinately.

1. P—K4, P—K4; 2. Kt—KB3, Kt—QB3; 3. P—Q4, P×P; 4. B—QB4, B—B4; 5. P—B3, P—Q6; 6. P—QKt4, B—Kt3; 7. P—QR4, P—QR3; 8. P—R5, B—R2; 9. Q—Kt3, Q—K2; 10. o—o, Kt—B3; 11. QKt—Q2, o—o; 12. B×QP, P—Q3; 13. P—Kt5, P×P; 14. Q×P, B—Q2, with a good game for Black.

TWO KNIGHTS' DEFENCE

An interesting way of varying from the Giuoco Piano by which Black sacrifices a pawn for a positional advantage.

1. P—K4, P—K4; 2. Kt—KB3, Kt—QB3; 3. B—B4, Kt—B3; 4. Kt—Kt5, P—Q4; 5. P×P, Kt—QR4; 6. B—Kt5 ch, P—B3; 7. P×P, P×P; 8. B—K2, P—KR3; 9. Kt—KB3, P—K5; 10. Kt—K5, B—Q3; 11. P—KB4, o—o; 12. Kt—QB3, R—K1; 13. o—o, B×Kt; 14. P×B, Q—Q5 ch; and Black regains his pawn with about equal chances.

VIENNA GAME

White first develops his QKt before attacking the centre by P—KB4.

1. P—K4, P—K4; 2. Kt—QB3, Kt—KB3; 3. P—B4, P—Q4; 4. BP×P, Kt×P; 5. Kt—B3, B—K2; 6. P—Q4, o—o; 7. B—Q3, P—KB4; 8. P×P e.p., B×P; 9. o—o, Kt—B3; 10. Kt×Kt, P×Kt; 11. B×P, Kt×P; 12. Kt—Kt5, B—B4; 13. P—B3, B×Kt; 14. QB×B, and the game is level.

The Half-open Defences

These are defences in which Black replies to 1. P—K4 with some move other than P—K4, and they are called half-open since they represent a halfway stage between the open and the close game. In fact, it would be fair to say that the centre, in about 50 per cent of the cases arising out of these defences is open.

Some of these defences are very popular indeed nowadays, so that it is essential to know something about them, and you would be well advised to choose one of them for yourself and practise, play and study it. Which you choose is entirely a matter of taste. The Sicilian is generally regarded as the best fighting defence; but the French is not far behind it in this respect. The Caro Kann is my own favourite, but is admittedly not to everybody's taste; whilst Alekhine's Defence well deserves being played at least now and then for its value as shock tactics.

SICILIAN DEFENCE

1. P—K4   P—QB4

Instead of contesting control of the centre point, K4, Black decides to counter-attack on the Q side. He attacks White's Q4 and, if White clears up this attack by playing P—Q4, then he hopes to gain pressure along the QB file.

2. Kt—KB3

Preparing to play P—Q4. Another scheme for White is the close system, by which he tries to keep the centre as closed as possible, whilst preparing a K-side attack, e.g. 2. Kt—QB3, Kt—QB3; 3. P—KKt3, P—KKt3; 4. B—Kt2, B—Kt2; 5. P—Q3, P—Q3; 6. B—K3, Kt—B3; 7. P—KR3, o—o; 8. Q—Q2, Kt—Q5; 9. QKt—K2, P—K4; 10. P—QB3, Kt—B3; 11. P—KB4, R—K1, with about a level game.

2. ....   P—Q3

The variation I give here is known as the Dragon Variation, but Black has a wide variety of choice. He can play (1) 2. ....., Kt—QB3; 3. P—Q4, P×P; 4. Kt×P, Kt—B3; 5. Kt—QB3, P—Q3; 6. B—KKt5 (the Richter-Rauser line); 6. ....., P—K3; 7. Q—Q2, P—QR3; 8. o—o—o, B—Q2; 9. P—B4, P—R3; 10. B—R4, Kt×P; 11. Q—K1, Kt—B3; 12. Kt—B5, Q—R4; 13. Kt×QP ch, B×Kt; 14. R×B, o—o—o, when on the whole one prefers White; or (2) 2. ....., Kt—QB3; 3. P—Q4, P×P; 4. Kt×P, Kt—B3; 5. Kt—QB3, P—Q3; 6. B—K2, P—K4 (the Boleslavsky system, in which Black obtains good play for his minor pieces at the cost of a backward QP);

7. Kt—Kt3, B—K2; 8. o—o, o—o; 9. B—B3, B—K3; 10. B—K3, Kt—QR4; 11. Kt×Kt, Q×Kt; 12. Q—Q2, KR—B1; 13. KR—Q1, Q—Kt5, with equality; or (3) 2. ...., P—K3 (not so fashionable as the other lines, but probably just as good); 3. P—Q4, P×P; 4. Kt×P, Kt—KB3; 5. Kt—QB3, P—Q3; 6. B—K2, B—K2; 7. o—o, Kt—B3; 8. B—K3, P—QR3; 9. P—B4, Q—B2; 10. Q—K1, o—o; 11. Q—Kt3, Kt×Kt; 12. B×Kt, P—QKt4; 13. P—QR3, B—Kt2, with about an equal game in which White's attack on the K side is balanced by Black's on the Q wing.

3. P—Q4	P×P
4. Kt×P	Kt—KB3
5. Kt—QB3	P—KKt3

The mark of the Dragon: Black's *fianchettoed* KB exerts strong pressure on the black squares of the long diagonal.

6. B—K2	B—Kt2
7. o—o	o—o
8. Kt—Kt3	Kt—B3
9. B—K3	B—K3
10. P—B4	Q—B1

With the idea of gaining control of two squares, KKt5 and QB5. Black can also obtain a satisfactory game by 10. ...., Kt—QR4.

11. Q—K1

So that if now 11. ...., B—Kt5 he can escape exchanges by 12. B—Q3.

11.	P—QR4
12. P—QR4	Kt—QKt5
13. Kt—Q4	B—Kt5

The position is level.

Of the other half-open defences the most important is the—

FRENCH DEFENCE

Black's idea is to induce White to advance his KP to K5 and then obtain a counter-attack by undermining its base, generally by attacking the QP with his QBP.

As in the Sicilian Defence, there are myriads of variations.
I give four main specimen lines.

The Orthodox Variation

1. P—K4, P—K3; 2. P—Q4, P—Q4; 3. Kt—QB3,
Kt—KB3; 4. B—Kt5, B—K2; 5. P—K5, KKt—Q2; 6. B×B,
Q×B; 7. Q—Q2, o—o; 8. P—B4, P—QB4; 9. Kt—B3,
Kt—QB3; 10. P×P, Kt×BP; 11. o—o—o, P—QR3; 12.
B—Q3, P—QKt4; 13. Kt—K2, B—Kt2; 14. Kt(B3)—Q4,
Kt×Kt; 15. Kt×Kt, and White has rather the better game.

Alekhine's Attack

1. P—K4, P—K3; 2. P—Q4, P—Q4; 3. Kt—QB3;
Kt—KB3; 4. B—Kt5, B—K2; 5. P—K5, KKt—Q2; 6.
P—KR4, P—QB4; 7. B×B, K×B; 8. P—B4, P×P; 9. Q×P,
Kt—QB3; 10. Q—Q2, P—QR3; 11. o—o—o, P—QKt4;
12. Kt—B3, Kt—Kt3, with equality.

The Winawer Variation

1. P—K4, P—K3; 2. P—Q4, P—Q4; 3. Kt—QB3, B—Kt5;
4. P—K5, P—QB4; 5. P—QR3, B×Kt ch; 6. P×B, Kt—K2;
7. Q—Kt4, Kt—B4; 8. B—Q3, P—KR4; 9. Q—R3, P×P;
10. Kt—B3, Kt—B3; 11. P—Kt4, and White has retained his
initiative.

Tarrasch Variation

1. P—K4, P—K3; 2. P—Q4, P—Q4; 3. Kt—Q2, P—QB4;
4. KP×P, KP×P; 5. B—Kt5 ch, B—Q2; 6. Q—K2 ch,
Q—K2; 7. B×B ch, Kt×B; 8. P×P, Kt×P; 9. Kt—Kt3,
Q×Q ch; 10. Kt×Q, Kt×Kt, with equality.

A very interesting defence was that introduced into master
chess by the late world champion Alexander Alekhine.

ALEKHINE'S DEFENCE

Black lures on White's pawns in the centre in the hope he
will overreach himself. White should accept the challenge and
advance his KP, but thereafter should be very careful not to
indulge in too many pawn moves.

A typical line is 1. P—K4, Kt—KB3; 2. P—K5, Kt—Q4; 3. P—Q4, P—Q3; 4. Kt—KB3, B—Kt5; 5. B—K2, P—K3; 6. o—o, B—K2; 7. P—B4, Kt—Kt3; 8. P×P, P×P; 9. Kt—B3, Kt—B3; 10. P—QKt3, o—o; 11. B—K3, P—Q4; 12. P—B5, Kt—Q2; 13. P—QKt4, Kt×KtP; 14. R—Kt1, Kt—QB3; 15. R×P, when White has an advantage.

During the last thirty years a highly modern defence, the Pirc Defence, has attained a popularity that is exceeded only by the Sicilian and possibly the French. Both the Pirc and its derivative, the Robatsch, are sophisticated systems that should really be left to the advanced player.

PIRC DEFENCE

This contains an idea not unlike Alekhine's Defence in that Black invites White to advance his centre pawns in the hope of striking back in the centre. Quite often his fianchettoed KB plays an important role in the counter-attack. A main line runs as follows:

1. P—K4, P—Q3; 2. P—Q4, Kt—KB3; 3. Kt—QB3, P-KKt3; 4. P—B4, B—Kt2; 5. Kt—B3. This is a quieter line. More ferocious, but not really so effective is 5. P—K5, P×P; and now White can choose between 6. QP×P, Q×Q ch; 7. K×Q, Kt—Kt5; and 6. BP×P, Kt—Q4; 7. B—QB4, Kt×Kt; 8. P×Kt, o—o.

5. ...., o—o; 6. P—K5, KKt—Q2; 7. B—B4, Kt—Kt3; 8. B—Kt3, Kt—B3; 9. o—o, Kt—R4; 10. Kt—K4, Kt×B; with equality.

ROBATSCH DEFENCE

Here Black fianchettoes his KB straightaway.

1. P—K4, P—KKt3; 2. P—Q4, B—Kt2; 3. P—QB4, P—Q3; 4. Kt—QB3, Kt—QB3; or he could transpose back to the Pirc by 4. ...., Kt—KB3.

5. P—Q5, Kt—Q5; 6. B—K3, P—QB4; 7. KKt—K2, Q—Kt3; 8. Q—Q2, B—Kt5; with a complicated tactical position that is poised on a knife-edge.

CARO KANN DEFENCE

A solid defence of which I give the two most popular lines

nowadays:

(1) 1. P—K4, P—QB3; 2. Kt—QB3, P—Q4; 3. Kt—B3,
B—Kt5; 4. P—KR3, B×Kt; 5. Q×B, P—K3; 6. P—Q3,
Kt—Q2; 7. B—K2, KKt—B3; 8. o—o, B—Q3; 9. B—Kt5,
o—o, with equality.

(2) 1. P—K4, P—QB3; 2. P—Q4, P—Q4; 3. Kt—QB3,
P×P; 4. Kt×P, B—B4; 5. Kt—Kt3, B—Kt3; 6. P—KR4,
P—KR3; 7. Kt—B3, Kt—Q2; 8. B—Q3, B×B; 9. Q×B,
Q—B2; 10. B—Q2, KKt—B3; 11. o—o—o, P—K3;
12. P—B4, o—o—o; 13. B—B3, B—Q3, and the position
is about even.

CENTRE-COUNTER DEFENCE

A bad defence, for the same reason that the Centre Game is
a bad opening; though in this case it is Black's Queen that is
brought out into the open too soon.

1. P—K4, P—Q4; 2. P×P, Q×P; 3. Kt—QB3, Q—QR4;
4. P—Q4, Kt—KB3; 5. Kt—B3, B—Kt5; 6. P—KR3,
B×Kt; 7. Q×B, P—B3; 8. B—Q2, QKt—Q2; 9. o—o—o,
P—K3; 10. B—QB4, Q—B2, with the better game for White.

THE QUEEN-SIDE OPENINGS

For some time now these have been much more popular
than the King-side openings since it is held (with some truth)
that they enable White to retain the initiative longer. It used
to be said that these openings were duller and less colourful
than the King-side openings, but this myth has been exploded
long ago. Such players as Bronstein and Keres have produced
time and again wonderful examples of imagination and power
with the Queen-side openings that are at least as good as those
created by the great masters of the previous century.

THE QUEEN'S GAMBIT

Just as the Ruy Lopez is the main regular opening on
the King side so the Queen's Gambit is the main Queen-
side opening. The objective too is the same—conquest of the
centre.

It should be pointed out here that this is not a true gambit,
since Black cannot hope to retain the pawn, and White would
be justified in feeling aggrieved if Black managed to do so

without suffering some disadvantage elsewhere.

1. P—Q4   P—Q4
2. P—QB4   P—K3

This leads to the Orthodox Defence, which gives Black a firm hold in the centre, but has the drawback of shutting in the Queen's Bishop. In fact, you will find that the development of this piece always causes Black trouble in the Q-side openings and this in turn will mean that it is difficult for the second player to get his QR into action.

Black may also accept the gambit, providing he does not try to cling on to his extra pawn. A modern example is the game Spassky–Keres from the Candidates' Tournament at Amsterdam, 1956: 2. ...., P×P; 3. Kt—KB3, Kt—KB3; 4. P—K3, P—K3; 5. B×P, P—B4; 6. o—o, P—QR3; 7. Q—K2, QKt—Q2; 8. Kt—B3, P—QKt4; 9. B—Kt3, B—Kt2; 10. R—Q1, P—Kt5; 11. Kt—QR4, Q—R4; 12. P—K4, Q—Kt4; 13. Q—K1, B×P; 14. Kt—K5, P—B5; 15. Kt×QBP, and now, instead of 15. ...., B—K2; 16. B—B4, o—o; 17. Kt—Q6, when White has a marked advantage, Black should play 15. ...., B—Q4; 16. Kt—K5, B—K2, with about an equal game.

3. Kt—QB3

Putting more pressure on Black's Q4, and indeed throughout the opening you will see White trying to induce Black to take off the QBP and thus give White control of K4.

3. ....   Kt—KB3
4. B—Kt5   QKt—Q2
5. P—K3

Why not 5. P×P, P×P; 6. Kt×P, winning a pawn? Because of 6. ...., Kt×Kt; 7. B×Q, B—Kt5 ch, when Black wins a piece!

5. ....   B—K2
6. Kt—B3   o—o
7. R—B1   P—B3

Giving further support to the centre and blocking the hidden attack by White's QR along the QB file.

8. B—Q3   P × P

At length Black does give up his hold on Q4 with the idea of freeing his position by exchanges.

9. B × P   Kt—Q4
10. B × B   Q × B
11. O—O   Kt × Kt
12. R × Kt   P—K4

This is the key move and the key position in the Orthodox Defence. Black opens up the diagonal for the development of his QB and the question is—how must White now proceed so as to keep up the pressure.

There are no less than seven reasonable lines.

57

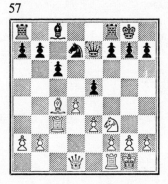

LINE ONE

13. P × P   Kt × P
14. Kt × Kt   Q × Kt
15. P—B4

This is known as the Rubinstein Variation, after the great Polish master, Akiba Rubinstein, who invented the line. The idea is to hinder the development of Black's Bishop by P—B5.

15. ....   Q—K5

Black has two alternatives:

(a) 15. ...., Q—B3; 16. P—B5, P—QKt4; 17. B—Q3, P—Kt5; 18. R—B5, R—K1; 19. Q—B1, B—Kt2; 20. P—KR3, with about a level game.

(b) 15. ...., Q—K2; 16. P—B5, P—QKt4; 17. B—Kt3, P—Kt5; 18. P—B6, P×P; 19. R×QBP, Q×P ch; 20. K—R1, with a fine attack for White.

16. Q—K2	B—B4
17. B—Q3	Q—Q4
18. P—K4	Q—Q5 ch
19. K—R1	KR—K1
20. R—B4	Q—Q2
21. Q—QB2	B—K3
22. R—QB3	

and White still has an attack.

LINE TWO (*see Diagram 57*)
13. P—K4

Planning to make a promising pawn sacrifice, but Black need not accept the offer.

13.	P×P
14. Kt×P	Kt—K4

White does get a dangerous attack after 14. ...., Q×P; 15. R—K1.

15. B—Kt3	P—QB4
16. Kt—K2	Kt—B3

with an equal position.

LINE THREE (*see Diagram 57*)
13. P—Q5

A refreshing change, but Black should still be able to cope with the threats, providing he reacts vigorously enough.

13.	P—K5
14. Kt—Q4	P—QB4
15. Kt—B5	Q—K4
16. Kt—Kt3	Kt—B3

and again the position is equal.

So far we have looked at pawn moves. The remaining lines are all concerned with piece moves in which White readjusts his position whilst waiting to see what Black will do. None of them really give so much chance for White as Line One.

LINE FOUR (*see Diagram 57*)

13.	B—Kt3	P×P
14.	P×P	Kt—B3
15.	R—K1	Q—Q3
16.	P—KR3	B—B4
17.	R—K5	B—K5

and Black has a good game.

LINE FIVE (*see Diagram 57*)

13. R—K1

So that, if Black exchanges pawns, then his Queen is attacked by White's Rook.

13.	....	P—K5
14.	Kt—Q2	K—R1

Preparing to advance his BP and so support his KP.

15.	Q—Kt1	P—KB4
16.	P—B3	Kt—B3
17.	P×P	P×P

with about an even game.

LINE SIX (*see Diagram 57*)

13. Q—B2

A move with a double purpose: it prepares to contest control of K4 and puts more pressure on the QB file.

13.	....	P—K5
14.	Kt—Q2	Kt—B3
15.	R—B1	K—R1
16.	P—QKt4	

The most interesting and the liveliest move here.

16.	....	Q×P
17.	Kt×P	Kt×Kt
18.	Q×Kt	

with advantages to White, since it is still difficult for Black to develop his Bishop usefully.

Line Seven (*see Diagram 57*)

13. Q—Kt1

A move invented by Capablanca with the idea of attacking on the Queen side as quickly as possible by P—QKt4.

13.	P × P
14. P × P	Kt—Kt3
15. R—K1	Q—B3
16. B—Kt3	B—K3
17. B × B	P × B
18. R(B3)—K3	QR—K1

with about an equal game.

In addition to the Orthodox Defence, there are a number of other important defences to the Queen's Gambit, and I give some sample lines below.

Albin Counter-gambit

A lively line that may be dangerous in the hands of an attacking player but one that is not really sound or good for Black.

1. P—Q4, P—Q4; 2. P—QB4, P—K4; 3. QP × P, P—Q5; 4. Kt—KB3, Kt—QB3; 5. QKt—Q2, B—KKt5; 6. P—KKt3, Q—Q2; 7. B—Kt2, o—o—o; 8. P—KR3, B—KB4; 9. P—R3, P—B3; 10. P × P, Kt × P; 11. P—QKt4, and White has the better game.

Cambridge Springs Defence

So called because it first became well known through being played at the great international tournament of Cambridge Springs in America which was won by Marshall, this defence has never been refuted.

1. P—Q4, P—Q4; 2. P—QB4, P—K3; 3. Kt—QB3, Kt—KB3; 4. B—Kt5, QKt—Q2; 5. P—K3, P—B3; 6. Kt—B3, Q—R4; 7. P × P, Kt × P; 8. Q—Q2, B—Kt5; 9. R—B1, o—o; 10. P—K4, Kt × Kt; 11. P × Kt, B—R6; 12. R—QKt1, P—K4; 13. B—Q3, R—K1; 14. o—o, P—QKt3; 15. Q—K2, B—Kt2; 16. KR—Q1, and White has a very slight advantage if any.

Why then, you might ask, is the Cambridge Springs not more often used nowadays? The answer is that by 6. P × P

White can avoid it and Black gets a rather lifeless game, as shown in the next line.

THE EXCHANGE VARIATION

1. P—Q4, P—Q4; 2. P—QB4, P—K3; 3. Kt—QB3, Kt—KB3; 4. B—Kt5, QKt—Q2; 5. P—K3, P—B3; 6. P×P, KP×P; 7. B—Q3, B—K2; 8. Q—B2, o—o; 9. Kt—B3, R—K1; 10. o—o, Kt—B1; 11. QR—Kt1 (preparing an attack on the Q side by P—QKt4–5); 11. ...., Kt—K5; 12. B×B, Q×B; 13. P—QKt4, with the better game for White.

LASKER'S DEFENCE

This tries to free Black's position by many exchanges, but White should still retain the initiative.

1. P—Q4, P—Q4; 2. P—QB4, P—K3; 3. Kt—QB3, Kt—KB3; 4. B—Kt5, B—K2; 5. P—K3, o—o; 6. Kt—B3, P—KR3; 7. B—R4, Kt—K5; 8. B×B, Q×B; 9. P×P, Kt×Kt; 10. P×Kt, P×P; 11. Q—Kt3, Q—Q3; 12. P—B4, P×P; 13. B×P, Kt—B3; 14. B—K2, B—K3; 15. Q—B3, Q—Kt5; 16. K—Q2, Q×Q ch; 17. K×Q, and White has the better game.

MANHATTAN VARIATION

A counter-attack that bears a strong resemblance to the Cambridge Springs Defence.

1. P—Q4, P—Q4; 2. P—QB4, P—K3; 3. Kt—QB3, Kt—KB3; 4. B—Kt5, QKt—Q2; 5. Kt—B3, B—Kt5; 6. P×P, P×P; 7. P—K3, P—B4; 8. B—Q3, P—B5; 9. B—B2, Q—R4; 10. o—o, B×Kt; 11. P×B, Q×BP; 12. Q—Kt1, and White has an attack that is well worth the pawn sacrificed.

It should be pointed out that Black cannot play the Manhattan if White plays 5. P—K3, since after 5. ...., B—Kt5; 6. P×P, P×P; 7. B—Q3, P—B4, White can blunt the edge of Black's counter-attack by 8. Kt—K2.

MERAN DEFENCE

Black develops his Q side early, and there is an interesting struggle for the initiative with about equal chances.

1. P—Q4, P—Q4; 2. P—QB4, P—QB3; 3. Kt—KB3, Kt—KB3; 4. Kt—B3, P—K3; 5. P—K3, QKt—Q2; 6. B—Q3,

P×P; 7. B×BP, P—QKt4; 8. B—Q3, P—QR3; 9. P—K4, P—B4; 10. P—K5, P×P; 11. Kt×KtP, Kt×P; 12. Kt×Kt, P×Kt; 13. Q—B3, B—Kt5 ch; 14. K—K2, R—QKt1; 15. Q—Kt3, Q—Q3; 16. Kt—B3, Q×Q; 17. RP×Q, B—Q3; 18. B—KB4, B×B; 19. P×B, B—Q2; 20. Kt×P, K—K2, with a level game.

RAGOSIN SYSTEM

Like the Manhattan, this can only be effective if White first plays an early Kt—KB3.

1. P—Q4, P—Q4; 2. P—QB4, P—K3; 3. Kt—QB3, Kt—KB3; 4. Kt—B3, B—Kt5; 5. P×P, P×P; 6. B—Kt5, Q—Q3; 7. Kt—Q2, P—B3; 8. P—K3, 0—0; 9. B—Q3, QKt—Q2; 10. 0—0, R—K1; 11. Q—B2, with rather the better game for White.

SEMI-TARRASCH DEFENCE

Again White must play Kt—KB3 on the fourth move to allow this equalising defence to be used.

1. P—Q4, P—Q4; 2. P—QB4, P—K3; 3. Kt—QB3, Kt—KB3; 4. Kt—B3, P—B4; 5. BP×P, Kt×P; 6. P—K3, Kt—QB3; 7. B—B4, P×P; 8. P×P, B—K2; 9. 0—0, 0—0; 10. R—K1, Kt×Kt; 11. P×Kt, P—QKt3; 12. B—Q3, B—Kt2; 13. Q—B2, P—Kt3; 14. B—KR6, R—K1; 15. Q—Q2, R—QB1; 16. QR—B1, B—B3; 17. Q—B4, B—Kt2, with about equal chances.

SLAV DEFENCE

There are many variations of this defence, which defends the centre by P—QB3 instead of P—K3, as in the Orthodox Defence. One of the most important lines is that in which Black temporarily accepts the gambit pawn.

1. P—Q4, P—Q4; 2. P—QB4, P—QB3; 3. Kt—KB3, Kt—B3; 4. Kt—B3, P×P; 5. P—QR4, B—B4; 6. P—K3, P—K3; 7. B×P, B—QKt5; 8. 0—0, QKt—Q2; 9. Q—K2, 0—0; 10. P—K4, B—Kt3; 11. B—Q3, B—KR4; 12. B—KB4, R—K1; 13. P—K5, Kt—Q4; 14. Kt×Kt, BP×Kt; 15. Q—K3, B—Kt3; 16. B—KKt5, B—K2, and the game is about even, though White has rather more space in which to manoeuvre.

TARRASCH DEFENCE

Black plays an early P—QB4 and achieves some freedom at the cost of an isolated Queen's pawn.

1. P—Q4, P—Q4; 2. P—QB4, P—K3; 3. Kt—QB3, P—QB4; 4. BP×P, KP×P; 5. Kt—B3, Kt—QB3; 6. P—KKt3, Kt—B3; 7. B—Kt2, B—K2; 8. o—o, o—o; 9. P×P, P—Q5; 10. Kt—QR4, B—B4; 11. B—B4, with advantage to White.

TARTAKOWER DEFENCE

This is really a variation of the Orthodox Defence in which Black *fianchettoes* his QB.

1. P—Q4, P—Q4; 2. P—QB4, P—K3; 3. Kt—QB3, Kt—KB3; 4. B—Kt5, B—K2; 5. P—K3, o—o; 6. Kt—B3, P—KR3; 7. B—R4, P—QKt3; 8. P×P, Kt×P; 9. B×B, Q×B; 10. Kt×Kt, P×Kt; 11. R—B1, B—K3; 12. Q—R4, P—QB4; 13. Q—R3, R—B1; 14. B—K2, Q—B1; 15. P×P, P×P; 16. o—o, Kt—Q2; 17. Kt—Q2, and White has some advantage.

TSCHIGORIN DEFENCE

Black makes a violent counter-attack that should not succeed.

1. P—Q4, P—Q4; 2. P—QB4, Kt—QB3; 3. Kt—QB3, P×P; 4. Kt—B3, Kt—B3; 5. P—K4, B—Kt5; 6. B—K3, B×Kt; 7. P×B, P—K4; 8. P—Q5, Kt—K2; 9. B×BP, and White has the better game.

THE VIENNA VARIATION

A fascinating line, full of combinative possibilities, but like so many of the variations given above, only possible when White has developed his KKt early.

1. P—Q4, P—Q4; 2. P—QB4, P—K3; 3. Kt—KB3, Kt—KB3; 4. B—Kt5, B—Kt5 ch; 5. Kt—B3, P×P; 6. P—K4, P—B4; 7. P—K5, P×P; 8. Q—R4 ch, Kt—B3; 9. o—o—o, B—Q2; 10. Kt—K4, B—K2; 11. P×Kt, P×P; 12. B—R4, R—QB1; 13. K—Kt1, Kt—QR4, and though White is a piece up, Black's attack and pawns are so strong that the position must be reckoned as about equal.

THE QUEEN'S PAWN DEFENCES

These are defences in which Black replies to 1. P—Q4 with some move other than P—Q4. The two most important are the King's Indian and the Nimzowitsch Defences and they are undoubtedly the most popular of all openings. Curiously enough they are both based on a counter-attack with the KB; but there the resemblance ends, and the plan of campaign for these two openings is about as different as it could possibly be.

The King's Indian Defence

Black *fianchettoes* his KB, and all the subsequent play is concerned with the way in which this Bishop's power can be increased—in short, this is a struggle for the black squares.

1.	P—Q4	Kt—KB3
2.	P—QB4	P—KKt3
3.	Kt—QB3	B—Kt2
4.	P—K4	P—Q3

Partly so as to prepare for P—K4 and partly so as to weaken any further advance of White's KP.

There are now four main paths for White.

58

I

5. P—B4

A terrifying advance known as the Four Pawns' Attack. Opinions as to its real worth have gone up and down over the years; at the moment of writing chances are held to be about equal.

5. ....   P—B4
6. P—Q5
If 6. P×P, Q—R4; 7. B—Q3, Q×BP; 8. Kt—B3, Kt—B3; 9. Q—K2, B—Kt5, with a good game for Black.

6. ....   o—o
7. Kt—B3   P—K3
Black sets himself to the task of breaking down White's impressive looking centre.

8. B—K2   P×P
9. KP×P   R—K1
10. o—o   Kt—Kt5
11. R—K1   B—B4
And not 11. ...., B—Q5 ch; 12. Kt×B, P×Kt; 13. Q×P, Q—R5; 14. B—Q2, when Black is too much behind in development.

12. P—KR3   Kt—K6
13. B×Kt   R×B
14. Q—Q2   R—K1
and the game is level.

II (see Diagram 58)

5. P—B3
Another fiercely attacking variation in which White intends to develop his Q side quickly, castle on that side and then launch an attack on Black's K side (where Black is practically forced to castle).

5. ....   o—o
6. B—K3   P—K4
7. P—Q5   Kt—R4
Black must counter-attack with P—KB4, and at the same time he bears in mind the possibility of Kt—B5.

8. Q—Q2   P—KB4

9. P×P   P×P
10. o—o—o   P—QR3

Preparing an attack on White's King by P—QKt4.

11. B—Kt5   Q—K1
12. Kt—R3   Kt—Q2
13. P—KKt4   P×P
14. P×P   Kt—B5
15. Kt—K4

Black has an overwhelming attack after 15. Kt×Kt, P×Kt; 16. B×P, P—Kt4. Note how powerful his KB has become in this variation.

15. ....   P—Kt4!
16. B×Kt   P×B
17. Kt(R3)—Kt5   Kt—K4

with the better game for Black. This was the opening of a game between Szabo and Bronstein in the Hungary–U.S.S.R. match at Budapest, 1955, which Black did in fact win.

III (see Diagram 58)

5. Kt—B3

A quieter line than the first two and one in which White first completes his K-side development before undertaking any attack.

5. ....   o—o
6. B—K2   P—K4
7. o—o   Kt—B3

More aggressive than 7. ...., QKt—Q2; though this also is quite playable.

8. P—Q5   Kt—K2
9. Kt—K1

So as to be able to advance his KBP and also with ideas of centralising the Kt—probably on Q3.

9. ....   Kt—Q2

Black must get in P—KB4—the plan which you will find occurring time and time again in the King's Indian.

10. B—K3	P—KB4
11. P—B3	P—B5
12. B—B2	P—KKt4
13. Kt—Q3	Kt—KB3
14. P—B5	Kt—Kt3

and we get a game in which White attacks on the Q side, whilst Black counters on the K side. On the whole one prefers Black.

IV (see Diagram 58)

5. P—KKt3

This is probably White's best line.

5.	o—o
6. B—Kt2	P—K4
7. KKt—K2	P×P

Also good is 7. ...., Kt—B3; and if 8. P—Q5, Kt—Q5.

8. Kt×P	Kt—B3
9. Kt×Kt	P×Kt
10. o—o	Kt—Q2
11. Q—B2	Q—B3
12. Kt—K2	R—K1
13. R—Kt1	Q—K2
14. B—Q2	Kt—B4
15. QR—K1	P—QR4

Not 15. ...., Kt×P because of 16. B×Kt, Q×B; 17. Kt—Q4.

16. P—Kt3   B—Kt5

with about an equal game. This was played by Bronstein as Black against Najdorf at Budapest, 1950. David Bronstein must be the greatest exponent of the King's Indian in the history of this defence.

The Nimzowitsch Defence

1. P—Q4	Kt—KB3
2. P—QB4	P—K3
3. Kt—QB3	B—Kt5

59

This is really an indirect way of holding back White's P—K4, or, if White does manage to get this move in, then Black hopes to get some advantage elsewhere, either by doubling White's QBPs or by gaining moves in development.

Of the many replies at White's disposal, four deserve to be called main lines.

I

4. P—QR3
A straightforward answer. White is prepared to have his pawns doubled so that in return he can build up a strong centre and, by means of the two Bishops, may obtain attacking chances on the K side.

4.	B × Kt ch
5. P × B	P—B4
6. P—K3	P—QKt3

A useful way of developing the Bishop, as it can go to either Kt2 or QR3, according to White's replies, whilst the pawn on Kt3 also provides a support for the QKt when this piece eventually lands on QR4.

7. B—Q3	B—Kt2
8. P—B3	o—o
9. Kt—K2	Kt—B3
10. P—K4	Kt—K1

An idea introduced by Capablanca so as to enable Black to block White's K side attacking chances by advancing his own KBP at the right moment.

11. O—O	Kt—R4
12. Kt—Kt3	P×P
13. P×P	R—B1
14. P—B4	

A forced pawn sacrifice by which, however, White hopes to gain time for his K-side attack.

14.	Kt×P
15. P—B5	P—B3
16. P—QR4	P—K4

and Black is safe enough.

II (see Diagram 59)

4. P—K3

The most popular line of the day and the one that causes Black the most trouble.

4.	P—B4
5. B—Q3	

After 5. P—QR3, Black can either transpose to Line 1 by B×Kt ch or else play 5. ...., P×P.

5.	P—Q4
6. Kt—B3	O—O
7. O—O	Kt—B3
8. P—QR3	B×Kt
9. P×B	QP×P
10. B×P	Q—B2

Black is preparing to play P—K4 and thus give his QB an outlet.

11. B—Q3	P—K4
12. Q—B2	R—K1
13. P—K4	P—B5
14. B×P	P×P
15. P×P	Kt—QR4

with a level game, since Black wins back his pawn after the coming exchange of Queens.

III (see Diagram 59)

4. Q—B2

White makes a direct attempt at controlling K4. This is also quite a popular line, but Black should get easy equality.

| 4. .... | o—o |
| 5. P—QR3 | |

Black has a fine game after 5. P—K4, P—Q3; 6. P—K5, P×P; 7. P×P, Kt—Kt5; 8. Kt—B3, Kt—QB3; 9. B—B4, P—B3.

5.	B×Kt ch
6. Q×B	P—QKt3
7. Kt—B3	B—Kt2
8. B—Kt5	P—Q3
9. P—K3	QKt—Q2
10. Q—B2	Q—K1
11. Kt—Q2	P—B4
12. P×P	KtP×P

and Black has a good game.

IV (see Diagram 59)

4. Q—Kt3

This line fails to deal with the main problem of the opening-control of K4, and is not so often seen as the three lines already given above.

4. ....   Kt—B3

An interesting move introduced by the British master, Milner-Barry, over forty years ago. Black both defends (his Bishop) and attacks (the QP)—an ideal plan.

5. Kt—B3	P—Q4
6. P—K3	o—o
7. P—QR3	P×P
8. B×P	B—Q3
9. Kt—QKt5	Kt—K5
10. Kt×B	P×Kt
11. o—o	P—QKt3

with a level game.

OTHER QUEEN'S PAWN DEFENCES

Benoni Defence

The defect of this defence is that Black loses ground in the centre and so gets a cramped game.

1. P—Q4, P—QB4; 2. P—Q5, P—K4; 3. P—K4, P—Q3;
4. B—Q3, Kt—K2; 5. Kt—K2, Kt—Kt3; 6. o—o, P—QR3;
7. P—QR4, B—K2; 8. Kt—R3, o—o; 9. Kt—QB4, Kt—Q2;
10. B—Q2, P—Kt3; 11. P—QB3, R—Kt1; 12. P—QKt4.
with the better game for White.

Benoni Defence Deferred

This is a much better line than the immediate Benoni, and
in many variations it results in a sort of King's Indian Defence.

1. P—Q4, Kt—KB3; 2. P—QB4, P—B4; 3. P—Q5,
P—KKt3; 4. Kt—QB3, B—Kt2; 5. P—KKt3, P—Q3;
6. B—Kt2, o—o; 7. Kt—B3, Kt—R3 (the Knight is to go to
B2 where it will help in a counter-attack by P—QKt4);
8. o—o, Kt—B2; 9. P—K4, P—QR3; 10. P—QR4, R—Kt1;
11. P—R5, P—QKt4; 12. P×P e.p., R×P, with equality.

Blumenfeld Counter-gambit

A lively counter-attack that is not, however, altogether
correct.

1. P—Q4, Kt—KB3; 2. P—QB4, P—K3; 3. Kt—KB3,
P—B4; 4. P—Q5, P—QKt4; 5. B—Kt5, KP×P; 6. P×QP,
P—KR3; 7. B×Kt, Q×B; 8. Q—B2, P—Q3; 9. P—K4,
P—R3; 10. P—QR4, P—Kt5; 11. QKt—Q2, B—Kt5;
12. B—K2, Kt—Q2; 13. Kt—KKt1, B×B; 14. Kt×B, and
White has the advantage.

Budapest Defence

Another interesting counter-attack in which Black offers up
his KP for the sake of development. White does best to give
back the pawn and satisfy himself with a positional advantage.

1. P—Q4, Kt—KB3; 2. P—QB4, P—K4; 3. P×P, Kt—Kt5
(White has much the better game after 3. ...., Kt—K5;
4. Q—B2, P—Q4; 5. P×P e.p., B—B4; 6. Kt—QB3, Kt×QP;
7. P—K4); 4. Kt—KB3, B—B4; 5. P—K3, Kt—QB3; 6.
B—K2, KKt×P(K4); 7. Kt—B3, P—Q3; 8. o—o, o—o;
9. P—QKt3, B—B4; 10. B—Kt2, R—K1; 11. Kt—QR4,
B—QKt3; 12. Kt×B, RP×Kt; 13. Kt—Q4, with the better
game for White.

Dutch Defence

Though this has been the favourite defence of some great

masters, particularly of former World Champion, Botvinnik, it is not as sound as, for instance, the King's Indian or the Nimzowitsch Defences. The drawback from which Black should never escape in this defence is his basically bad pawn structure.

1. P—Q4, P—KB4; 2. P—QB4, P—K3; 3. P—KKt3, Kt—KB3; 4. B—Kt2, B—K2; 5. Kt—KB3, o—o; 6. o—o, P—Q3; 7. Kt—B3, Q—K1; 8. R—K1, Q—Kt3; 9. P—K4, Kt×P; 10. Kt×Kt, P×Kt; 11. R×P, Kt—B3 (not 11. ...., Q×R; 12. Kt—R4, winning the Queen); 12. R—K1, and White has the advantage owing to the backward KP.

Grunfeld Defence

This good defence is an offshoot of the King's Indian, the difference being that Black plays an early P—Q4.

1. P—Q4, Kt—KB3; 2. P—QB4, P—KKt3; 3. Kt—QB3, P—Q4; 4. P×P, Kt×P; 5. P—K4, Kt×Kt; 6. P×Kt, P—QB4; 7. B—QB4, B—Kt2; 8. Kt—K2, P×P; 9. P×P, Kt—B3; 10. B—K3, o—o; 11. o—o, B—Kt5; 12. P—B3, Kt—R4, with about a level game. If now 13. B—Q3, B—K3, or if 13. B—Q5, B—B1.

Old Indian Defence

A rather colourless defence in which Black invites exchanges by an early P—Q3 and P—K4.

1. P—Q4, Kt—KB3; 2. P—QB4, P—Q3; 3. Kt—QB3, P—K4; 4. P×P (or White can transpose into a King's Indian by 4. Kt—B3, P—KKt3); 4. ...., P×P; 5. Q×Q ch, K×Q; 6. Kt—B3, KKt—Q2; 7. P—KKt3, P—KB3; 8. B—Kt2, P—B3; 9. o—o, Kt—Kt3; 10. P—Kt3, B—K3; 11. B—K3, QKt—Q2, with equality.

Queen's Indian Defence

A fine defence that Black can only play when White plays an early Kt—KB3. There are two main lines, depending on whether White plays Kt—KB3 on the second or the third move: (1) 1. P—Q4, Kt—KB3; 2. Kt—KB3, P—QKt3; 3. P—KKt3, B—Kt2; 4. B—Kt2, P—B4; 5. o—o, P×P; 6. Kt×P, B×B; 7. K×B, P—Kt3; 8. P—QB4, Q—B1; 9. P—Kt3, B—Kt2; 10. Kt—QB3, Q—Kt2 ch; 11. P—B3, P—Q4; 12. P×P, Kt×P; 13. Kt×Kt, Q×Kt; 14. B—Kt2, o—o, and Black has a good game.

(2) 1. P—Q4, Kt—KB3; 2. P—QB4, P—K3; 3. Kt—KB3, P—QKt3; 4. P—KKt3, B—Kt2; 5. B—Kt2, B—K2; 6. o—o, o—o; 7. Kt—B3, Kt—K5; 8. Q—B2, Kt×Kt; 9. Q×Kt, P—KB4; 10. P—Kt3, B—KB3; 11. B—Kt2, Q—B1; 12. Q—Q2, P—Q3; 13. Kt—K1, Kt—Q2; 14. R—Q1, P—QR4, with a level game.

Other Queen-side Openings

We are now concerned with a block of highly modern openings which need a great deal of experience to play and which you would do well to avoid until you have acquired that experience.

Catalan System

White strengthens his pressure on the point Q5 (after, for example, playing a Queen's Gambit) by means of a King's *Fianchetto*.

1. P—Q4, P—Q4; 2. P—QB4, P—K3; 3. P—KKt3, Kt—KB3; 4. B—Kt2, P×P; 5. Q—R4 ch, QKt—Q2; 6. Q×BP, P—QR3; 7. Q—B2, P—B4; 8. Kt—KB3, P—QKt4; 9. P—QR4, B—Kt2; 10. o—o, R—B1; 11. RP×P, RP×P; 12. Q—Kt3, Q—Kt3, with about a level game.

English Opening

Though this is an old opening, it still belongs to this modern group, as the spirit in which it is played nowadays is very different from that of a hundred years ago. White concentrates his attack on the white squares, usually by means of a King's *Fianchetto*.

1. P—QB4, P—K4; 2. Kt—QB3, Kt—KB3; 3. P—KKt3, P—Q4; 4. P×P, Kt×P; 5. B—Kt2, Kt—Kt3; 6. Kt—B3, Kt—B3; 7. o—o, B—K2; 8. P—Q3, o—o; 9. B—K3, P—B4; 10. Kt—QR4, P—B5; 11. B—B5, B—Kt5; 12. R—B1, and White has some advantage.

Réti's Opening

White refrains from any attempt at occupying the centre for some time, and hopes to gain an advantage by attacking Black's centre after the latter has advanced his pawns there.

1. Kt—KB3, P—Q4; 2. P—B4, P—Q5; 3. P—K3, Kt—QB3;
4. P×P, Kt×P; 5. Kt×Kt, Q×Kt; 6. Kt—B3, P—K4;
7. P—Q3, P—QB3; 8. B—K3, Q—Q3; 9. P—Q4, P×P;
10. Q×P, Q×Q; 11. B×Q, Kt—B3, with equality.

There are a number of specialised openings in which White has a definite plan in mind from the very start and in which the pawn formation is a rigid one. Now, whilst it is a very good thing to play with a plan in mind, it is just as bad to stick to it rigidly without considering how conditions may change or what effect the opponent's moves may have on one's ideas.

This stiffness of outlook is the main drawback of the following three openings:

Bird's Opening

A sort of Dutch Defence with a move in hand and, curiously enough, perhaps worse than when played with Black.

1. P—KB4, P—Q4; 2. Kt—KB3, Kt—KB3; 3. P—K3, P—KKt3; 4. P—QKt3, B—Kt2; 5. B—Kt2, o—o; 6. B—K2, P—B4; 7. o—o, Kt—B3; 8. Kt—K5, Q—B2; 9. P—Q3, P—Kt3; 10. Kt—Q2, B—Kt2; 11. QKt—B3, QR—Q1, with a good game for Black.

Colle System

White plays an early P—K3 and assembles his pieces so as to get the maximum amount of effect from an eventual P—K4.

1. P—Q4, P—Q4; 2. Kt—KB3, Kt—KB3; 3. P—K3, P—B4; 4. QKt—Q2, P—KKt3; 5. P—B3, QKt—Q2; 6. B—Q3, B—Kt2; 7. o—o, o—o; 8. Q—K2, R—K1; 9. P—K4, P—K4; 10. P×KP, KKt×P; 11. Kt×Kt, P×Kt; 12. B×P, Kt×P, with a fine game for Black.

Stonewall System

This unites the defects of the two previous openings.

1. P—Q4, P—Q4; 2. P—K3, Kt—KB3; 3. B—Q3, P—B4; 4. P—QB3, Kt—B3; 5. P—KB4, B—Kt5; 6. Kt—B3, P—K3; 7. o—o, B—Q3; 8. QKt—Q2, P×P; 9. BP×P, o—o; 10. Q—K1, R—B1; 11. Kt—K5, B—KB4, with advantage to Black.

CHAPTER V

THE MIDDLE-GAME

THE middle-game arises naturally out of the opening. This may seem a simple obvious statement to you, but there is more in it than first meets the eye. The point is that the type of attack or defence that you must use depends entirely on the nature of the opening. It is no use trying to build up a fine game by accumulating small advantages in a violent gambit type of opening. Do that, and before you know where you are your opponent will have mated you. Equally, do not try to win off-hand by a sweeping or abrupt combination in a close positional game. For in that case you will find you have ruined your own position just as quickly as, in the first example, you have been mated.

Let me illustrate my point by the following game played at the great International Tournament of Groningen in 1946:

White: H. Steiner. *Black:* Najdorf

1. P—Q4, Kt—KB3; 2. P—QB4, P—K3; 3. Kt—QB3, B—Kt5; 4. Q—B2, P—Q3; 5. P—QR3, B×Kt ch; 6. Q×B, P—QR4; 7. Q—KKt3, o—o; 8. B—R6, Kt—K1; 9. P—K4, P—K4; 10. Kt—B3, P×P; 11. Kt×P, Q—B3; 12. B—K3, P—B4; 13. P—K5, Q×P; 14. Q×Q, P×Q; 15. Kt—B3, Kt—Q2, and Black had won a pawn, this advantage being enough for him to force a win in another twenty odd moves.

Now, what went wrong with this game? White got into trouble solely because he played as though he had started off with an opening like the Giuoco or as though he had played 1. P—K4 and Black had replied with a French Defence. The moves 7, 8 and 9 were all part and parcel of this faulty plan. Instead, White should have continued quietly but firmly, with 7. P—KKt3 and 8. B—Kt2.

This was the wrong way. Now let us see how a similar plan of K-side attack, involving the same attacking move, Q—KKt3, succeeded when used in the right circumstances. Played at the Interzonal Tournament at Gothenburg, 1955:

QUEEN'S PAWN, QUEEN'S INDIAN DEFENCE

White: Keres. *Black:* Spassky

1. P—Q4, Kt—KB3; 2. P—QB4, P—K3; 3. Kt—KB3, P—QKt3; 4. P—K3, B—Kt2; 5. B—Q3, B—K2; 6. o—o, o—o; 7. P—QKt3, P—Q4; 8. B—Kt2, QKt—Q2; 9. Kt—B3, P—B4; 10. Q—K2, QP×P; 11. KtP×P, Q—B2; 12. QR—Q1 (note how carefully White prepares for the attack; no dashing out with his Queen before all his other pieces are fully developed and in co-operation); 12. ....., QR—Q1; 13. P—Q5, P—QR3; 14. P×P, P×P; 15. Kt—KKt5, Q—B3; 16. P—B4, P—R3; 17. Kt—B3, Q—B2; 18. Kt—KR4, B—Q3; 19. B—Kt1, KR—K1; 20. Q—KB2, Kt—B1; 21. Q—Kt3, Kt—R4; 22. Q—R3, Kt—B3; 23. Kt—Kt6, P—K4; 24. Kt—Q5, B×Kt; 25. P×P, B×KP; 26. Kt×B, B—K3; 27. Q—Kt3, R×R; 28. R×R, P—QKt4; 29. R—KB1, Kt(B3)—Q2; 30. Q×P ch, resigns. Because he loses much material after 30. ....., K×Q; 31. Kt×Kt dis. ch, K—Kt1; 32. Kt—B6 ch, K—B2; 33. Kt—Q5 dis. ch.

The moral of all this is that you must *form a plan that fits the position.* But I must emphasise that it is vitally necessary to form a plan. How many games I have seen lost by young players (by old, too, for that matter) through aimless drifting and just move-to-move play. The best type of chess and the best type of game is that in which every move fits in to form a perfect pattern.

Now you may say, "It's all very well talking about forming plans, but how do I form them? In fact, is it possible to learn how to play the middle game at all?" The answer is that, just as in the openings and the endings, practice and experience count for a lot, but all the same one can learn a great deal from examples and from basic principles. There are typical attacks and typical defences; standard ways of attacking and defending the King side or the Queen side. There are even typical combinations which, though they may not be exactly the same move for move yet are concerned with the same idea.

For instance, look at the final combination in the justly

famous game which Morphy won against the Duke of Bruns-
wick and Count Isouard in consultation during an operatic
performance at Paris in 1858:

PHILIDOR'S DEFENCE

1. P—K4, P—K4; 2. Kt—KB3, P—Q3; 3. P—Q4, B—Kt5;
4. P×P, B×Kt; 5. Q×B, P×P; 6. B—QB4, Kt—KB3;
7. Q—QKt3, Q—K2; 8. Kt—B3, P—B3; 9. B—KKt5,
P—Kt4; 10. Kt×P, P×Kt; 11. B×KtP ch, QKt—Q2;
12. 0—0—0, R—Q1; 13. R×Kt, R×R; 14. R—Q1, Q—K3;
15. B×R ch, Kt×B; 16. Q—Kt8 ch, Kt×Q; 17. R—Q8 mate.

60   Black (Stoltz)

White (Spielmann) to play

Diagram 60 (above) shows a position that arose after the
seventeenth move in the tournament at Bled, 1931. Spielmann,
momentarily forgetful of the end of the Morphy game, played
18. P—K4, and then had a long, hard struggle before he won.
Bearing in mind the Morphy combination, we can see in a
flash that 18. QR—Q1 would have won off-hand.

Or, for a more complicated example, take Diagram 61,
from a game played at Teplitz-Schonau, 1922. White's position
is such that his pieces on the Q side find it practically impossible
to get over to the other side so as to protect the King. Black
can therefore sacrifice a Rook for a mating attack as follows:
17. ...., R×P; 18. K×R, Q×P ch; 19. K—R1, Kt—B3;
20. R—K2, Q×KtP; 21. Kt—Kt1, Kt—R4; 22. Q—Q2,
B—Q2; 23. R—B2, Q—R5 ch; 24. K—Kt1, B—Kt6; 25.
B—B3, B×R ch; 26. Q×B, P—Kt6; 27. Q—KKt2, R—KB1;

28. B—K1, R×B ch; 29. K×B, P—K4; 30. K—Kt1, B—Kt5;
31. B×P, Kt×B; 32. R—K1, Kt—B4; 33. Q—KB2, Q—Kt4;
34. QP×P, B—B6 dis. ch; 35. K—B1, Kt—Kt6 ch, and White
resigns.

61   Black (Dr. Tartakower)
to play

White (Maroczy)

Thirty-five years later the young Danish grandmaster,
Bent Larsen, had exactly the same idea at the European Zonal
Tournament at Wageningen, 1957 (Diagram 62). Again came
the Rook sacrifice, 22. ...., R×P ch; 23. P×R, Q×P ch;
24. K—Kt1, B—R6; 25. P—K3, R—KB1; 26. Q—K2,
R—B3; 27. B—Q5 ch, K—B1, and White resigns, since he is
in a mating net after, say 28. Kt—K1, Q—Kt4 ch; 29. K—R2,
R—R3.

62   Black (Larsen) to play

White (Dr. Troianescu)

Clearly, such ideas do not repeat themselves in exactly the
same details; but the basic idea is the same for all that. Bearing

this in mind, let us now have a look at some typical ways of attacking the King. I have chosen examples which, I hope, are both instructive and entertaining.

ATTACKS ON THE KING-SIDE

Breaking through the pawn barrier

Since the best defence of a castled King is an unmoved line of pawns, it follows that it is easier to break through such a line when one or more of the pawns have been moved. In fact, in Diagram 63 practically no break-through is necessary, so far have the pawns been moved in front of the King. Black is able to force a quick win by 45. ...., R—R6; 46. Q—Kt2, Q—Q6; 47. P×P, Kt—K5; 48. P×P, Q—K6 ch; 49. K—B1, R—B6 ch, White resigns.

63 Black (Keres) to play

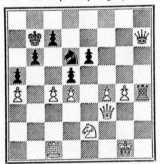

White (Gligoric)
Zürich, 1953

64 Black (Polugaievsky)

White (Gurgenidze) to play
Tiflis, 1956

Violence is necessary in Diagram 64, where White breaks through by means of a Rook sacrifice; 34. R×P ch, P×R; 35. R×P ch, R×R; 36. Q×R(Kt6) ch, K—R1; 37. Q—R6 ch, K—Kt1; 38. Q—Kt5 ch, K—R1; 39. Kt—K7, resigns, as in order to prevent mate Black must give up his Queen.

In Diagram 65 it is the fact that the KBP has been moved that enables White to break up Black's K side. 30. R×P ch, K×R (or 30. ...., K—R1; 31. P—K6, Q×B; 32. R—K7 dis. ch, P—Q5; 33. R×R ch, K—Kt2; 34. Q—Kt3 ch, followed by mate in two moves. Note that 31. ...., P—Q5;

is met by 32. B—K5); 31. P—K6 dis. ch, K—R3; 32. Q—R3 ch, K—Kt2; 33. B—K5 ch, resigns.

65   Black (Antoshin)

White (Tolush) to play
XXIV U.S.S.R. Championship, 1957

66   Black (Talvik)

White (Goglidze) to play
Tiflis, 1928

Again the advanced KBP is the source of the trouble in Diagram 66; but here White uses it to open up an attack on the file. 20. P—KKt4, P—Kt3; 21. P × P, KtP × P (21. . . . ., KP × P does not lose so quickly as the text move; but it does still lose, owing to White's 22. P—K6!); 22. R—Kt1 ch, K—R1; 23. Q—Kt2, Q—B2; 24. B × P, Q—Q2 (if 24. . . . ., P × B; 25. P—K6); 25. B—R6, B—KR5; 26. B × P, resigns. If 26. . . . ., Q × B; 27. B—Kt7 ch, K—Kt1; 28. B—B6 dis. ch, with mate to follow.

And now a typical assault by means of a pawn advance. In Diagram 67 White can force a complete break-through by

67   Black (Tchukaev)

White (Korchnoi) to play
Tiflis, 1956

means of a piece sacrifice, as follows: 29. P—Kt6, P—R3; 30. Kt×RP, P×Kt; 31. B×P, R×R; 32. R×R, R—Kt1; 33. R—B7, Kt—Kt2; 34. Q—B4, resigns. Black cannot avoid mate.

When one is faced by an unmoved pawn chain, the problem is a little different. How can the opponent be persuaded to move his pawns or allow them to be broken up? A typical sacrifice to achieve just this purpose is shown in Diagram 68.

68   Black (Prochorovitch)

White (Estrin) to play
Moscow Championship, 1957

White plays 25. R—B6, P×R; 26. P×P, Q—B1; 27. Q—Q3 (note how Black is induced to move yet another pawn); 27. ...., P—R3; 28. Q—Kt3 ch, K—R2; 29. B—K3, R—B5; 30. B×P, resigns. Black can only choose between 30. ...., R×R; 31. B×Q and 30. ...., Q×B; 31. Q—Kt7, mate.

Another very common way of breaking through an un-moved pawn chain is by sacrificing a piece (usually a Bishop) on KR7. To be effective, such a sacrifice should take place when the opponent has not got a Knight either on his KB3 or his KB1, or when the Knight cannot reach such a position in one move. This can be seen in Diagram 69 where White wins by 1. B×P ch, K×B; 2. Q—R5 ch, K—Kt1; 3. R×P, Q×R; 4. P—Kt6, and Black has nothing better than to sur-render his Queen by 4. ...., Q×KtP, after which he is quite lost.

The Belgian master, E. Colle, specialised in sacrifices of this type, and his games are full of instructive examples of the Bishop sacrifice. Here is one which works even with a Knight on Black's KB3, though the Knight itself cannot move owing to a pin:

69 Black (Tchekhover)

White (Kasparian)
U.S.S.R., 1936

COLLE SYSTEM

White: Colle.   *Black:* Buerger

Hastings, 1928–9

1. P—Q4, Kt—KB3; 2. Kt—KB3, P—Q4; 3. P—K3, P—K3; 4. B—Q3, B—K2 (Black plays the opening too passively, which explains why White gets such a strong attack. Here at least he should have played 4. ...., P—B4); 5. QKt—Q2, o—o; 6. o—o, QKt—Q2; 7. P—K4, P×P; 8. Kt×P, Kt×Kt; 9. B×Kt, Kt—B3; 10. B—Q3, P—B4; 11. P×P, B×P; 12. B—KKt5, B—K2; 13. Q—K2, Q—B2; 14. QR—Q1, R—Q1; 15. Kt—K5, B—Q2; 16. B×P ch, K×B (Black loses the exchange after 16. ...., Kt×B; 17. B×B); 17. B×Kt, B×B; 18. Q—R5 ch, K—Kt1; 19. Q×P ch, K—R2; 20. R—Q3, resigns, as he has no way of preventing R—R3 ch.

One can often get a position with doubled KBPs in which the King may seem quite safe from attack; and then, in a flash, the safety disappears and the King is wide open to a mating assault. An example is Diagram 70, where White wins by 20. Kt—K5, Q—K2 (if 20. ...., P×Kt; 21. Q—Kt5 ch, K—R1; 22. Q—B6 ch, K—Kt1; 23. R—K3, KR—K1; 24. Q—R6, K—R1; 25. R—KKt3, and Black is mated in two moves); 21. Kt—Kt4, R—KKt1; 22. Kt—R6 (threatening

not only the Rook, but also the Queen—by Kt—B5 ch);
22. ...., Q—B2; 23. Kt×R, R×Kt; 24. P—QKt3, K—R1;
25. Q—R6, R—Kt3; 26. Q—R4, Kt—Q2; 27. R—K3,
Q—R4; 28. R—R3, Kt—B1; 29. R—Kt3, Q×P; 30. R×R,
Kt×R; 31. Q×BP ch, K—Kt1; 32. Q—B3, Q—B7; 33.
Q—Q3, resigns. Naturally, Black could play on for some time
if he wished to do so; but in such an open position the advantage
of the exchange is sure to be decisive.

70   Black (Stahlberg)   71   Black (Padevsky) to play

White (Smyslov) to play   White (Szabo)
Zürich, 1953   Uppsala, 1956

Holes in the King-side

Advancing the King-side pawns, in particular the KKtP, is
often a risky process. In so doing one creates holes in the
position that may prove fatal, especially if one cannot control
the vital squares with one's pieces. It follows that, though a
King's *fianchetto* may be a very strong defence to the King
whilst the Bishop is there, once this piece has been exchanged
the *fianchetto* formation may well be a fatal one. A simple
example is shown in Diagram 71, where White's game might
be defensible if there were still a Bishop on KKt2. As it is,
Black wins almost at once by 29. ...., B×P; 30. P×B, R×P
ch, White resigns. It should be observed that the player of the
White pieces is not the Hungarian grandmaster Szabo, but a
player of the same name who represented Roumania in the
Students' World Team Championship at Uppsala in Sweden.
    The want of the KB is perhaps even clearer in Diagram 72,
where White won by 37. R×P ch, P×R (or 37. ...., B×R;

38. Q×Kt ch, B—B2; 39. Q—KB6); 38. P—R7 ch, K×P;
39. Q×B ch, Kt—Kt2; 40. K—B2, resigns.

72   Black (Petrosian)

White (Taimanov) to play
Zürich, 1953

Next, a typical combination based on the same weakness by
which White forces a mating finish. White's problem in Diagram 73 is how to clear the lines for the action of his QB so as
to form a mating net. He solves it by 21. P—B5, KP×P;
22. B—KKt5, Kt—K3; 23. B—B6, P—KB5; 24. Q×RP ch,
resigns.

73   Black (Pilnik)   74 Black (Nezmetdinov) to play

White (Olafsson) to play   White (Gurgenidze)
Match, Reykjavik, 1957   XXIV U.S.S.R. Championship, 1957

Finally, in Diagram 74 we see the hole on KKt2 enabling
Black to shatter White's King-side. Here, too, the weakness of
White's KB2 is also apparent. Black wins by 24. ...., R×P;
25. K×R (or 25. Q×R, R—KB1; 26. Q—K1, R—B8 ch;

27. Q×R, B×Kt ch); 25. ...., Q—R7 ch; 26. K—K1,
Q×P ch; 27. K—Q2, Q×Kt; 28. Kt—Q5, Q—Kt4 ch,
White resigns.

SACRIFICES OF ELIMINATION

Very often when conducting a King-side attack you will
find that one piece above all prevents your attack from winning
through. Usually, the piece concerned is a minor piece (either
Bishop or Knight) and it will pay you to eliminate it by a
sacrifice of a piece of greater value.

In Diagram 75 White has succeeded in opening up the KR
file for his major pieces; but the *fianchettoed* Bishop still stands
in his way and it is even worth his while to give up both Rooks

75   Black (Abramavicius)   76   Black (Nedeljkovic)

White (K. Richter) to play   White (Karaklaic) to play
Hamburg, 1930   Yugoslav Championship, 1957

if only he can eliminate the KB. White wins by 19. R—R8 ch,
B×R; 20. R×B ch, K×R; 21. Q—R1 ch, Kt—R2 (or 21. ....,
K—Kt1; 22. Kt—B6 ch, Q×Kt; 23. P×Q, B×B; 24. Q—R6,
Kt—K3; 25. Kt—Kt5, R×P ch; 26. K—Q1); 22. Kt—B6,
K—Kt2; 23. Q—R6 ch, followed by mate next move.

Another example of the same theme is shown in Diagram 76,
though here the defending Bishop is first diverted from its best
defensive post. White wins by 27. R—R8 ch, B×R; 28. Q—R7
ch, K—B1; 29. Q×B ch, K—K2; 30. Q—Kt7 ch, Kt—B2;
31. Q×Kt ch, K—Q3; 32. Kt—K4 mate.

The King has been chased out into the centre in Diagram 77;
but here too the KB is the main stumbling block and must be
eliminated. White wins by 17. R×B, Kt×R; 18. R—K1,

Q—Q3 (if 18. ...., Kt—B3; 19. R—K8 ch, R×R; 20. Q×R ch, K—B2; 21. Kt—Q5 ch); 19. Q—Kt7, Kt—Kt3; 20. Kt—K5, R—B1; 21. Kt—B7 ch, R×Kt; 22. Q×R, Q—Q7; 23. R—K8 ch, K—B2; 24. Kt—Q5 ch, K—Kt1; and Black resigns without waiting for White's reply; for White mates by 25. R×B ch, K×R; 26. Q—K8. Black would also have been mated after 24. ...., K—B3; 25. R—K6 ch, P×R; 26. Q—B7.

77   Black (Ujtelky)

White (Alster) to play
Czechoslovakian Championship, 1956

Other pieces also are liable to this treatment. In Diagram 78 it is the QKt that is the linch-pin of Black's defence and it is

78   Black (Toran)

White (Clarke) to play
Hastings, 1956-7

essential to eliminate it before White can strike at Black's KB2. So White plays 16. R×Kt, Q×R; 17. Kt×P, Q—B2; 18. Kt×P, P—Kt3 (if 18. ...., Kt—B3; 19. B×Kt, P×B;

20. Q—Kt4, mate); 19. Kt—Q5, B×Kt; 20. B×B, R—R2;
21. Kt—Q6 dis. ch, K—Kt2; 22. R×R, resigns; because of
22. ...., K×R; 23. Q—B3 ch, K—Kt2; 24. Kt—K8 ch.

In Diagram 79 Black's attack along the KKt file is thwarted
by the White Queen. If he can either eliminate this piece or

79   Black (Petrov) to play

White (Rellstab)
Kemeri, 1937

divert it temporarily from the KB3 square, then he can force
home his mating attack. This he does by 25. ...., B×P ch;
26. Q×B, R—Kt6; when White resigns because of the mate
on KR3.

CONCENTRATION OF FORCES

One thing has, I hope, emerged from the examples given
above. Attacks are only successful when they are backed by
adequate forces. Obviously, to try to attack a large number of
pieces with a small force is both useless and costly and before
delivering an assault one must concentrate the forces as much
as possible.

Here is an ideal example of what I mean from the Candidates' Tournament at Zürich in 1953:

QUEEN'S PAWN, KING'S INDIAN DEFENCE

White: Taimanov.   *Black:* Najdorf

1. P—Q4, Kt—KB3; 2. P—QB4, P—KKt3; 3. Kt—QB3,
B—Kt2; 4. P—K4, P—Q3; 5. Kt—B3, o—o; 6. B—K2,
P—K4; 7. o—o, Kt—B3; 8. P—Q5, Kt—K2; 9. Kt—K1,

Kt—Q2; 10. B—K3, P—KB4; 11. P—B3, P—B5; 12. B—B2, P—KKt4; 13. Kt—Q3, Kt—KB3; 14. P—B5, Kt—Kt3; 15. R—B1, R—B2; 16. R—B2, B—B1; 17. P×P, P×P; 18. Q—Q2, P—Kt5; 19. KR—B1, P—Kt6; 20. P×P, P×P; 21. B×KtP, Kt—R4; 22. B—R2, B—K2; 23. Kt—Kt1, B—Q2 (note how Black first develops his Queen-side before engaging forces on the other wing); 24. Q—K1, B—KKt4; 25. Kt—Q2, B—K6 ch; 26. K—R1, Q—Kt4; 27. B—B1, QR—KB1; 28. R—Q1, P—Kt4 (so as to prevent White from counter-attacking by Kt—QB4); 29. P—R4, P—QR3; 30. P×P, P×P; 31. R—B7, R—Kt2; 32. Kt—Kt3, Kt—R5; 33. R—B2, B—R6! (a beautiful move, after which every single one of Black's pieces is concentrated on the attack; in addition to the KtP, Black is threatening to capture the BP by R×BP); 34. Q—K2 (if 34. P×B, Q—Kt8 ch; 35. B×Q, R×B ch; 36. K—R2, Kt×P mate); 34. ...., Kt×KtP; 35. B×Kt, B×B ch; 36. Q×B, Q—R5 (threatening not only the Queen, but also Kt—Kt6 ch); 37. Q×R ch, K×Q; 38. R—Kt2 ch, K—R1; 39. Kt—K1, Kt—B5; 40. R—Kt3, B—B7; 41. R—Kt4, Q—R6; 42. Kt—Q2, P—R4; 43. R—Kt5, and White resigns, since after 43. ...., R—KKt1; 44. R×R ch, K×R he has no means of parrying the mate on Kt2 (after Black's B×Kt).

THE CENTRE AND CENTRALISATION

Closely bound up with the question of concentration of forces is that of the centre and its control. Once you have your pieces massed in the centre it becomes very much easier to concentrate them in attack in the desired direction. Moreover, you will find that your major pieces (the Queen and the Rooks) have much more scope for action when placed in the centre than when tucked away on the flank. So decentralisation of such pieces as the Queen or the Rooks should be shunned like the plague.

A characteristic example of the dangers involved is shown in Diagram 80. Here Black should centralise his QKt by playing Kt(R3)—B2, instead of which he decentralises his Queen by 17. ...., Q—Kt5; and swift punishment follows: 18. Kt—K4, P—KB4; 19. Kt(K4)—Kt5 ch, P×Kt; 20. Kt×P ch, K—R1; 21. B—KB3, Q—Q5; 22. Kt×B, Q×KtP;

23. Q×Q, B×Q; 24. R—Kt1, B×P; 25. R×P, B—Kt5;
26. B×B, Kt(R3)×B; 27. R×RP, R—R1; 28. R(K1)—R1,
Kt—Kt3; 29. Kt—B4, resigns.

80   Black (Bonham) to play

White (Golombek)
Paignton, 1957

On the other hand, how powerful are the centralised pieces
as opposed to the decentralised appears in Diagram 81,
where the superiority of Black's centrally placed Knight as
contrasted with White's unfortunate piece on R3 is made

81   Black (Golombek) to play

White (Van Steenis)
Beverwijk, 1949

clear by 23. ...., Kt—K4; 24. B—R7, R×R; 25. P×R,
P—R6; 26. B—K4, K—B2; 27. B—R1, K—Kt1; 28. P—KB4,
B—R5 ch; 29. K—B1, Kt×P; 30. R—Q4, Q×R; White
resigns. Certainly the Black Queen could not be more centralised (or more powerful) than it is here!

Now, just as it pays to have more pieces in the centre than your opponent, so it is a great advantage to have more pawns there. Quite often you will see a player trying to establish a strong line of pawns on the flank whilst neglecting the centre, and in nearly every case this is bad strategy. An example of this is the following game, in which Black's preponderance of pawns in the centre exerts a strong influence on the whole course of play:

QUEEN'S PAWN, NIMZOWITSCH DEFENCE

White: Beni.   *Black:* Golombek

Hamburg, 1955

1. P—Q4, Kt—KB3; 2. P—QB4, P—K3; 3. Kt—QB3, B—Kt5; 4. P—K3, P—B4; 5. Kt—K2, P—Q4; 6. P—QR3, BP×P; 7. KP×P, B—K2; 8. P—B5, o—o; 9. Kt—Kt3, B—Q2; 10. B—K2, P—QKt3; 11. P—Kt4, P×P; 12. QP×P (the mistake mentioned above; instead, he should play 12. KtP×P); 12. ...., Q—B2; 13. P—B4, R—Q1; 14. B—K3, B—K1 (the centre pawns are revealed as more dangerous than the flank ones; Black threatens 15. ...., P—Q5; 16. B×P, Kt—B3; 17. Kt—Kt5, Q×KBP); 15. B—B3, P—QR4; 16. QKt—K2, P×P; 17. P×P, R×R; 18. Q×R, Kt—B3; 19. Q—Kt1, R—Kt1; 20. o—o (the flank pawns must be abandoned; if 20. B—Q2, B×P; or 20. P—Kt5, Q—R4 ch); 20. ...., R×P; 21. Q—Q3, Kt—QR4; 22. Kt—Q4, B×P; 23. Kt(Kt3)—K2, Q—Kt3; 24. R—B1, B—Kt4; 25. Q—B3, R—B5; 26. Q—Kt2, R×R ch; 27. Q×R, B×Kt(K7); 28. B×B, Kt—Kt6, White resigns.

So we see the power of a mass of pawns in the centre; but even one single pawn can advance most effectively along central lines. Take the position in Diagram 82; apparently White's QP is rather weak and cannot advance, but see how quickly it does speed forward: 16. P—Q5, Kt—R4 (not 16. ...., Q×QP; 17. Kt—B6 ch, winning the Queen) 17. P—Q6, B—Q1; 18. Kt—B3, Q—R3; 19. QR—Q1, B—Kt5; 20. R—Q4, B—B4; 21. Q—R4, R—Kt1; 22. R—Q5, B—K3; 23. R—K5, P—Kt3; 24. P—Q7, P—QKt4; 25. R×P, R×R; 26. Q×R, Q×Q; 27. Kt×Q, P—R3; 28. Kt—B3, B×P (now the QP has gone, but in order to dispose of it

Black has been compelled to weaken his Queen-side pawns and White, as soon becomes clear, still controls the centre files); 29. R—Q1, B—B1; 30. Kt—K4, B—K2; 31. B—B5, B×B; 32. Kt×B, B—B4; 33. Kt×P, R—K1; 34. B—B3, Kt—Kt6;

82   Black (Stahlberg)

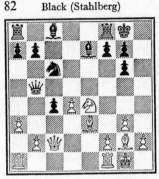

White (Reshevsky) to play
Zürich, 1953

35. K—Kt2, B—B7; 36. R—Q7, B—B4; 37. R—Q1, B—B7;
38. R—Q7, B—B4; 39. R—Q6, B—K3; 40. Kt—B7, R—K2;
41. Kt×B, resigns.

HINTS ON MIDDLE-GAME TACTICS

Whilst the middle-game is a realm in which an almost bewildering number of different possibilities arise, there are certain familiar tactics which recur again and again. I could give a very large quantity of examples, but for this there is neither space nor need, and I limit myself to some typical modern specimens.

The Seventh Rank

Conquest of the seventh rank with Rooks and (or) with Queen is usually equivalent to winning the game; for this is the vital rank on which most of the pawns stand and also a rank that very much concerns the safety of the King.

It is the King that suffers as a result of the occupation of the seventh rank in my first example (Diagram 83). The finish was: 28. P×B, R—K7 ch; 29. K—B1 (or 29. K—Kt1, Kt×P; 30. Q—Q8 ch, K—Kt2; 31. B—R6 ch, K—R2; 32. Q—KB8,

Q—Kt8 ch, followed by mate); 29. ...., Q—B7; 30. B—Q2, Q—Q8 ch; 31. B—K1, R—B7 ch; 32. K—Kt1, Q—K7; White resigns, as he is mated after 33. B×R, Q×B ch; 34. K—R1, Q—B8 ch; 35. Kt—Kt1, Kt—B7.

83   Black (Boleslavsky)

White (Livshin) to play
Semi-final, XXIV U.S.S.R. Championship, 1956

With two Rooks on the seventh, the usual way to win is to threaten mate by moving one Rook along the rank as in Diagram 84, where White won by 31. R—R7 ch, K—Kt1;

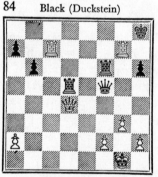

84   Black (Duckstein)

White (Szabo) to play
Wageningen, 1957

32. R(B7)—Kt7 ch, K—B1; 33. R×QRP, K—Kt1; 34. R(KR7)—Kt7 ch, K—R1 (or 34. ...., K—B1; 35. R(Kt7)—B7 ch, R×R; 36. Q—R8 mate); 35. R(Kt7)—KB7, resigns.

More subtle is my last example of this type, in which White

forces the win by less violent but extremely clever means:
36. P—B5, P×P ch; 37. K×P, Kt—K3; 38. P—R5 (threatening P—Kt6); 38. ...., Kt—Q5 ch; 39. K—K4, Kt—K3;
40. P—R6 ch, K—Kt1; 41. P—Kt6! Kt—Q1 (if 41. ....,
P×P; 42. P—R7 ch, K—R1; 43. Kt×P mate); 42. Kt—Q7,
R—K1 ch; 43. K—Q5, resigns.

85   Black (Penrose)

White (Smyslov) to play
Amsterdam, 1954

The Back Rank

The danger about the back rank is the sudden invasion by
an enemy force to give mate. This is putting it in its simplest
terms, and there are almost untold variations on this theme.
Take, for instance, the following neat little game:

QUEEN'S PAWN, BENONI DEFENCE DEFERRED

White: Orbaan. *Black:* Larsen

Wageningen, 1957

1. P—Q4, Kt—KB3; 2. Kt—KB3, P—B4; 3. P×P, P—K3;
4. P—K3, B×P; 5. B—K2, o—o; 6. o—o, P—Q4; 7. P—QKt3,
Kt—B3; 8. B—Kt2, Q—K2; 9. P—B4, P×P; 10. B×P,
P—K4; 11. B—Kt5 (not a good manœuvre; it would be
better to give up a pawn for counter-play by 11. P—K4,
Kt×P; 12. Q—K2); 11. ...., P—K5; 12. B×QKt, P×B;
13. Kt—K5, B—Q3; 14. Kt×QBP, B×P ch; 15. K×B,
Q—B2 ch; 16. K—Kt1, Q×Kt; 17. Q—Q4, B—R3; 18.
R—B1, Q—K3; 19. Kt—R3, KR—K1; 20. R—B7 (better
is 20. R—B5, and if QR—Q1; 21. Q—K5); 20. ...., QR—Q1;
21. Q×RP, Kt—Kt5; 22. R—B2 (now his second rank is

adequately guarded, but not his back rank, as Black's reply shows); 22. ...., Q—Q3; White resigns.

Quite often, however, the danger on the back rank is not apparent, since either pawns or pieces are in the way and seem to prevent any invasion by the enemy. Then comes a combination that clears the way out of the blue. Here are two examples, both won by Keres, in which in the first he makes a decisive gain in material, whilst in the other he forces mate:

86   Black (Keres) to play

White (Geller)
Zürich, 1953

Here all would be well if only there were an outlet for the White King from the back rank. As it is, Black won by 21. ....., Kt—Kt5; 22. R—K3, Kt×P; 23. P—R3, B×Kt; 24. P×B, Kt×P; 25. B—Q7, R—Q1; 26. B—B5, P—KKt3; 27. B—Q3, Kt—Q8, White resigns.

87   Black (Alekhine)

White (Keres) to play
Margate, 1937

Again the loser suffers from having no outlet for his King and here the end is swifter, as White wins by 1. Q×B ch, whereupon Black resigns, since he is mated after 1. .... R×Q, 2. R—K8 ch, R—Q1; 3. R×R.

The Open File

We have seen something of the way in which an open file can be used earlier on in this chapter under the heading of King-side attacks. But an open file can also be of great use in operations other than those concerned with a direct attack on the King. It can provide a jumping off point for attack along another file or rank and it may also be used for maintaining consistent pressure against the opponent's pawns and pieces. I give two examples from the games of the Soviet grand-master, Taimanov, who seems to specialise in this type of operation.

In Diagram 88 he has reduced his opponent almost to a *zugzwang* position, and the game continued 29. P—QR4

88   Black (Taimanov)

White (Unzicker) to play
Stockholm, 1952

(if 29. R×P, Q—B3; 30. R—K1, R×B; 31. Q×R, Q×Q; 32. R×Q, Kt—K7 ch); 29. ...., P—Kt5; 30. K—R1, Q—B3, White resigns. There is no way of averting Black's B—KB5, followed by Kt—B4.

The next position (Diagram 89) shows him again in posses-sion of the open QB file, but this time White's game is more solid and takes much more to break down: 23. ...., P—R4 (whilst White is pinned down to defence on the Queen-side, Black prepares an attack on the other wing); 24. P—Q5, R(B1)—B5; 25. R—Q1 (if 25. P×KP, Q×KP; 26. P×P, R×B; 27. QR×R, R×R; 28. Q×Q, R×R ch); 25. ...., KP×P; 26. B—Q2, Q—KB3; 27. QR—Kt1, P—R5; 28. Q—R4, Q—B4; 29. Q×RP, B—B1; 30. Q—Kt8, P—Kt4; 31. P×RP, P×KRP; 32. Q—B4, Q×Q; 33. P×Q, P—Q5; 34. P—Kt3, R—B3; 35. P×P, P—B4; 36. P—R3, R—QR3; 37. R(Kt1)—B1, R×R; 38. R×R, R—R7 (Black has converted his mastery of the open QB file to control of the seventh

89   Black (Taimanov) to play

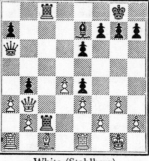

White (Stahlberg)
Zürich, 1953

rank, and although for the moment he is a pawn down, his positional advantage is so great that he must win in a few moves); 39. B—K1, R—Kt7; 40. K—Kt2, R×P; 41. R—B8, R—Kt8; 42. B—Q2, P—K6, White resigns, because of 43. P×P, R—Kt7, winning the Bishop.

Whilst on the subject of files, here is a very useful hint about a matter that crops up time and time again. Always try to get your Rook opposite the enemy Queen; or, conversely, when your opponent puts his Rook opposite your Queen you should sense danger and move your Queen away as soon as possible. This applies just as much if there are pawns or other pieces in between the Rook and the Queen; the hidden danger may emerge into the open at any moment. Take, for example, the following painful occurrence from the Dublin International Tournament, 1956:

QUEEN'S PAWN, KING'S INDIAN DEFENCE

White: Golombek. *Black:* Reid

1. P—Q4, Kt—KB3; 2. P—QB4, P—KKt3; 3. Kt—QB3, B—Kt2; 4. P—K4, P—Q3; 5. P—B3, o—o; 6. B—K3, P—K4; 7. KKt—K2, QKt—Q2; 8. Q—Q2, P×P; 9. Kt×P, Kt—B4; 10. B—K2, P—QR3; 11. o—o, B—Q2; 12. QR—Q1, Q—K2; 13. KR—K1 (with three pieces in the way, you might think the Queen was safe from the Rook, but only another four moves prove otherwise); 13. ...., Kt—K3; 14. Kt—B2, KR—K1; 15. B—B1, QR—Q1; 16. Kt—Q5, Kt×Kt? (he has not yet realised the danger to his Queen; here Q—B1 was the only way of avoiding loss of material); 17. KP×Kt, Kt—B1; 18. B—Kt5, and lo and behold the Queen (and, of course, the game) is lost in an open board.

To reinforce the lesson, look at another example (Diagram 90). White played 21. R—K1, and Black, instead of realising

90   Black (Pilnik)

White (Panno) to play
Amsterdam, 1956

the danger and playing his Queen away to B1, replied 21. ...., QR—Q1, then came 22. Kt—Q5, P×Kt; 23. KP×P, Q—B1; 24. P×Kt, R×P; 25. B×P, R×R; 26. Q×R, R—K1; 27. Q—B3, and White had won a pawn, and eventually did win the game as well.

The Exchange

Whilst it is quite certain that in all normal cases a Rook is worth more than a minor piece, you should always be alive to the possibility of an exchange sacrifice in order to bring off a winning combination. It is in fact quite surprising how often one meets this in present-day chess. An example is the following neat little game from the 23rd Soviet Championship:

RUY LOPEZ, MORPHY DEFENCE

White: Boleslavsky.   *Black:* Cholmov

1. P—K4, P—K4; 2. Kt—KB3, Kt—QB3; 3. B—Kt5, P—QR3; 4. B—R4, Kt—B3; 5. o—o, B—K2; 6. R—K1, P—QKt4; 7. B—Kt3, o—o; 8. P—B3, P—Q3; 9. P—KR3, Kt—QR4; 10. B—B2, P—B4; 11. P—Q4, Q—B2; 12. QKt—Q2, B—Q2; 13. Kt—B1, KR—K1; 14. Kt—K3, B—KB1; 15. P—QKt4, BP×QP; 16. P×P, Kt—B3; 17. B—Kt2, Q—Q1; 18. P—R3, P×P; 19. Kt×P, KKt×P; 20. Kt—Q5, Q—R5? (hastening disaster; he must play 20. ...., Kt—Kt4, even though White has a very strong attack after 21. P—B4, Kt—K3; 22. Kt—B5); 21. R×Kt!, R×R; 22. Kt—KB3, resigns.

Curiously enough, in the same tournament the same player demonstrated the force of this sacrifice in a still subtler way (Diagram 91). Play proceeded 17. ...., R×Kt! (the point about this sacrifice is that as a result Black gains full control of

91   Black (Boleslavsky) to play

White (Chasin)

the centre); 18. P×R, Kt×P; 19. B—K1, P—B4; 20. R—Q3, B—KB3; 21. Q—R2, R—B1; 22. K—R1, P—R3; 23. P—R3, K—R2; 24. K—R2, P—Kt4; 25. P×P, B×P; 26. Q—K2, B—KB3; 27. P—Kt3, B—QR1 (threatening Q—QKt2);

28. Q—R5, R—KKt1; 29. B—Q2, Kt×B; 30. R×Kt,
B—K4; 31. R—Q3, R—Kt4; 32. Q—K2, Q—KKt2; 33.
Q—K1 (if 33. Kt×KP, R×P; 34. Kt×Q, R—Kt7 db. ch,
etc.); 33. ...., Q—Kt3; 34. Kt—K2, P—B5; 35. R—B3,
P×P ch; 36. Kt×P, B×R; 37. R×B, R×Kt; 38. R×R,
Q×R ch; 39. Q×Q, B×Q ch; 40. K×B, K—Kt3; 41.
K—B4, K—B3; 42. K—K4, K—Kt4; 43. P—B4, P×P;
44. P—Kt4, K—B3, White resigns, since the Black King can
easily catch the remote QRP.

PAWNS

I often think that it is in the way you move (or refrain from
moving) your pawns that the true art of the middle-game lies.
You must be very careful about moving your pawns. Remember that, unlike pieces, the moves of pawns cannot be adjusted
in any way except forwards, and that in consequence a pawn
move may well shape the course of the whole game.

Thus, one rash pawn move in front of one's King can ruin
the game. Take the following brevity from the 1957 Dutch
Open Championship:

RÉTI OPENING

White: Van Weezel.   *Black:* Roessel

1. Kt—KB3, Kt—KB3; 2. P—KKt3, P—KKt3; 3. B—Kt2,
B—Kt2; 4. o—o, o—o; 5. P—B4, P—Q3; 6. Kt—B3, P—K4;
7. P—Q3, Kt—K1; 8. B—Q2, P—KR3? (bad; he should play
Kt—QB3); 9. P—K4, P—KB4 (still worse; he should still
play Kt—QB3); 10. Kt—KR4, Q—B3; 11. Kt—Q5, resigns.
For if 11. ...., Q—B2; 12. Kt×KtP.

In this case the loser sinned through moving his pawns
rashly; but still worse is the habit of making useless pawn
moves. Quite a large number of those games in which sudden
death is dealt out are the result of useless pawn moves, e.g.
the following from a zonal tournament at Ashchabad, 1957:

SICILIAN DEFENCE

White: Muchitdinov.   *Black:* Nurmumedov

1. P—K4, P—QB4; 2. Kt—KB3, Kt—QB3; 3. P—Q4,
P×P; 4. Kt×P, Kt—B3; 5. Kt—QB3, P—Q3; 6. B—QB4,

P—QR3?; 7. Kt×Kt, P×Kt; 8. P—K5, P×P?; 9. B×P ch, resigns.

Having given the evil side of pawn moves, I feel I must also say something about the good aspects. Nothing gives one a greater sense of potential force than the advanced passed pawn, and how great an influence it can exert on the course of the game is shown by the next example: (Diagram 92). White now created his passed pawn by 16. Kt×QP, Kt×B; 17. Kt×R, B×Kt? (bad; better is 17. ...., Kt×KP ch; 18. Kt×Kt, R×Kt, though even then White's strong passed pawn gives him an advantage); 18. P×Kt, B—Q5; 19. P—Q6, Q×Kt;

92   Black (Saidy)

White (Bertholdt) to play
Uppsala, 1956

20. P—Q7, Q—Q1; 21. B×R, Q×B; 22. KR—Q1 (as a matter of arithmetical fact, Black, with three minor pieces for the two Rooks, has an advantage in material; but the advanced passed pawn is too strong); 22. ...., Kt—Q4; 23. P—K3, P—B5; 24. Q—R3, B—B4; 25. Q—B3, B—Q3; 26. R×Kt, resigns.

Nimzowitsch's vivid phrase about the pawn's lust to expand is further illustrated by the following position (Diagram 93). White won by 32. P—B5!, B—R4 (if 32. ...., B×P; 33. Kt—R6 ch, K—R1; 34. Q×Q ch, K×Q; 35. Kt×B ch, and wins; or if 32. ...., R×Kt; 33. Q×Q ch, K×Q; 34. R×R, R×P; 35. R—Q7 ch, R—B2; 36. R(Kt4)—Q4, and wins); 33. P—B6!, Q—Kt3; 34. P—B7 ch!, R×P; 35. Kt—R6 ch, Q×Kt; 36. R—Q8 ch, R—B1; 37. R×R ch, Q×R; 38. R×R, Q—Q3; 39. R—K1, B—B2; 40. Q—R5, Q×P; 41. Q—Q8 ch,

K—Kt2, and here the game was adjourned, but Black resigned without resuming play, on account of the following
variations: 42. Q—Q4 ch, and if 42. ...., K—B1; 43. Q—B5
ch, K—Kt2; 44. R—KKt1, or if 42. ...., K—R3; 43. R—R1
ch, B—R4; 44. R—KKt1, Q—B2; 45. Q—B6 ch, B—Kt3;
46. R—R1 ch, followed by mate.

93   Black (Matanovic)

White (Sliwa) to play
Sofia, 1957

DEFENCE

I have talked much of attack so far, since clearly it is better
to play the game in an aggressive spirit; but it is also important
to know how to defend a position, since one cannot be attacking
all the time.

Just as in attack, so in defence the supreme lesson to be
learned is to keep the pieces concentrated in co-operation. In
order to defend successfully, it is vital to keep one's forces
linked together.

An example of this successful co-operation is seen in the
tenth game of the 1957 World Championship match between
Smyslov and Botvinnik: (Diagram 94). This is a typical
attacking position arising out of the Ruy Lopez. White played
18. P—QR4, Q—Kt2; 19. P×P, P×P; 20. P—R4, B—Q3;
21. Kt—Q5, Kt—KR4; 22. Kt—B3, P—B3; 23. B—R6,
R—B2; 24. KR—Q1, B—Kt5; 25. Q—K3, Kt—Kt2; 26.
R—Q2, Kt—K1; 27. Kt—R2, B—K3; 28. Q—Kt3, K—R1;
29. QR—Q1, R(Q1)—Q2 (notice how all the pieces are linked

together to defend vital squares); 30. Kt—B1, B—Kt1; 31.
B—K3, Kt—R4 (and now he prefers to counter-attack rather
than defend the QBP); 32. B×P, Kt—B5; 33. R—K2, Kt×P;
34. R—Kt1, Q—B3; 35. B—Kt4, Kt—B5; 36. P—R5, P—Kt4;
37. Kt(B1)—K3, Kt(K1)—Q3; 38. B×Kt, Kt×B; 39. B—Q3,
R—QKt2; 40. R(K2)—Kt2, P—R3; 41. Q—B3, B—R2; 42.

94   Black (Botvinnik)

White (Smyslov) to play
Moscow, 1957

P—B4, P×P; 43. R×R, Kt×R; 44. Kt×QBP, K—Kt2;
45. B—K2, B—Q5; 46. Kt(Q5)—K3, B×Kt(K6); 47. Kt×B,
Kt—Q3, drawn.

That the ideal form of defence is counter-attack was shown
by this last example, and it appears even more clearly in
another game from the same match—the seventh (Diagram 95).

95 Black (Smyslov) to play

White (Botvinnik)
Moscow, 1957

Here Black has to find a way of meeting the two threats Q×B and QR—Q1, and he plays 19. ...., Q—K5!, meeting a threat by a counter-threat, after which Botvinnik could find nothing better than to go for the draw by 20. Kt—B3, Q—B3; 21. Kt—Kt5, Q—Kt3; 22. Q×Q, P×Q; 23. KR—Q1, Kt—K5, draw agreed.

CHAPTER VI

CHAMPIONSHIP CHESS

THERE are a large number of opportunities, both for boys and girls, to play in championship chess, and these opportunities should be seized with both hands, as the hard practical play involved in battling your way through such an event is the best possible means of improving your strength as a player. In fact, practically all the leading players of the country have at one time or other taken part in these competitions, and many boy champions have gone on to win major events in adult company.

The chief events are perhaps the British Boys' and Girls' Championships, both of which are run annually by the British Chess Federation; but almost as important are the more local events, such as the London Boys' Championship held every Christmas by the London Chess League and the Birmingham and District's annual Junior Chess Congress. Both these cities also run school chess leagues, and the London School's Chess League and the Birmingham and District Junior League are very thriving organisations. I doubt whether anything in chess is as thrilling and satisfying as being a member of a winning team in such an event, and I myself am more proud at having played for the champion side three years in succession in the London Schools' League than of having won the British Championship thrice.

On the whole, there has been a steady rise in the quality of play in these events in the last fifty years—that is, since my time as a boy player—more being known by the young players about the openings and the endings than used to be the case.

Here are two typical examples of good games from boys' championship chess tournaments.

The following game was awarded the prize for the best game in the London Boys' Championship (under eighteen) Tournament, 1956–7. The notes given in brackets are by the winner, my own comments being unbracketed.

GIUOCO PIANO

White: P. D. Stephens.   *Black:* L. Sunderland

1. P—K4	P—K4
2. Kt—KB3	Kt—QB3
3. B—B4	B—B4
4. P—B3	Kt—B3
5. P—Q4	P×P
6. P×P	B—Kt5 ch
7. B—Q2	B×B ch
8. QKt×B	P—Q4

(This is Black's best reply.)

For remarks about the earlier moves see Chapter IV on the openings, p. 52. The thrust with the QP is a typically freeing manœuvre for Black, by which at one fell swoop he destroys White's powerful centre and develops his own Queen-side pieces.

Note that if 8. ...., Kt×KP, White should reply 9. P—Q5 (not 9. Kt×Kt, P—Q4); 9. ...., Kt×Kt; 10. Q×Kt, Kt—K2; 11. P—Q6, P×P; 12. 0—0—0, with a strong attack in return for the pawn sacrificed.

9. B—Kt5

(This relinquishes the initiative since Black need not keep the pawn. 9. P×P, KKt×P; 10. Q—Kt3, is met by 10. ...., Q—K2 ch.)

The first note is fully justified. Its idea is that Black can capture the KP and then not bother with retaining his extra pawn. Instead of clinging on to his material, he can complete his development whilst White is consuming time to make the number of pawns level. Note that another basic reason for the badness of B—Kt5 is that it involves moving the same piece twice in the early stages of the game without due reason or necessity.

However, the variation given by the winner in his next note contains a mistake that should be carefully noted and avoided. After 9. P×P, KKt×P; 10. Q—Kt3, Kt(B3)—K2 is correct, as given in Chapter IV, p. 52. For after 10. ...., Q—K2 ch; 11. K—Q1 Black has a lost game. The two threats are R—K1 and B×Kt. If 11. ...., Kt—R4; 12. Q—Kt5 ch wins a piece; whilst if 11. ...., Kt—B5; 12. R—K1, B—K3; 13. P—Kt3 and again White wins a piece.

9. ....   P×P
10. Kt—K5   0—0

(Better than 10. ...., B—Q2; 11. Kt×B, Q×Kt; 12. Q—R4, followed by R—QB1, when Black is under pressure.)

An excellent move, of which the great Paul Morphy would have heartily approved. Black profits both in development and position by giving back the pawn. This is an idea well worth bearing in mind, as it occurs time and again in the early middle-game.

11. Kt×Kt   P×Kt
12. B×P   R—Kt1
13. Kt—Kt3   R—Kt3
14. R—QB1   Q—Q3

Observe how all along Black is gaining time and developing his pieces by attacking White's advanced and rather displaced Bishop.

15. Q—B2   B—R3

(Keeping White's King permanently in the centre.)

The fact that the King is so placed is equivalent to having a lost game for White. It is vitally important in such open positions to be able to tuck away the King in safety on one or other of the wings. Here, however, 0—0—0 is impossible, since the Queen's Rook has been moved, and now 0—0 is out of the question.

All that Black has to do, therefore, is to open up a few more lines and the White King will succumb to attack.

96

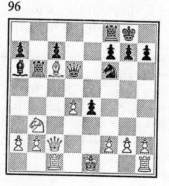

16. Q—B5

(16. B×P is met by 16. ...., Kt×B; 17. Q×Kt, Q—Kt5 ch; 18. K—Q1, R—K3; and White has no defence against B—K7 ch and KR—K1.)

This note needs a little expansion, since the variation is not immediately conclusive. It would continue 19. Q—R4, KR—K1; 20. K—B2, B—B5; 21. Q—Kt3, B×Kt ch; 22. Q×B, Q×P, and Black has a clearly won position. All the same, this would have been White's best chance of putting up a fight, since as played he loses very quickly.

16. ....   Q—B5
17. P—Q5   Kt—Kt5

(Preventing Q—K3.)

And threatening P—K6.

18. Q—Q4??

The double query marks are those given by the winner, and this move fully deserves them. It is a fatal mistake. He must keep his pieces in co-operation.

Note that after 18. P—KR3, P—K6 still wins. For if then 19. P×Kt, Q×P ch; 20. K—Q1, Q—K7, mate.

White's only way of maintaining some sort of struggle was by 18. Q—B2, P—K6; 19. P—B3.

18. ....   R×Kt!
19. R—Q1   R—K6 ch!

White resigns.

(The Queen is lost after 20. K—Q2, R—Q6 db. ch.)

A fine game which is a credit to the winner and from which plenty of instruction can be gained.

The next game was also awarded a best game prize in the same Boys' Congress, but this time in the Intermediate (under-sixteen) class. Again the notes given in brackets are those of the winner.

RÉTI OPENING

White: L. J. Wallace.   *Black:* K. M. Oliff

1. Kt—KB3   Kt—KB3
2. P—KKt3   P—KKt3
3. P—QKt3

As a rule, two *fianchettos* constitute a luxury that one player can hardly afford. The idea of placing the Bishop on a long diagonal and in a position where it is not liable to attack by enemy pawns or pieces is a most attractive one, but it demands time, and if White indulges in such a waste of moves, then he is likely to lose the initiative; if Black does it, then he may be penalised still more severely by loss of space, the difference in the nature of the penalties being due to the fact that White is, or should be, always slightly ahead on time, as he is the first to move in the game.

So here I prefer a pawn move that would at once develop a piece, or pieces, and control the centre—either 3. P—B4 or 3. P—Q4.

3. ....   B—Kt2
4. B—QKt2   P—B4

Note that Black wisely refrains from repeating White's error by a double *fianchetto* and instead plays a sensible pawn move that gives him a hold on the central Q5 square.

5. B—Kt2   P—Q4
6. P—B4

(This allows Black to shut in White's QB. Best was 6. P—Q4.)

Black's criticism of this move is not altogether justified; for, after 6. ...., P—Q5; 7. P—K3, Kt—B3; 8. P×P, P×P; 9. o—o, White would have quite a lot of play along the open King file. In any case, it will be seen that Black does not at once avail himself of the opportunity of advancing his pawn to Q5.

6. ....   o—o
7. o—o

What is wrong with White's play in this game is that he is moving and thinking rather too obviously in the kind of opening where it is essential that a player must think deeply and for himself. If you just go on playing mechanically without giving much thought to the consequences, you are bound to come unstuck in any opening; but the punishment is even heavier in this particularly complicated style of game.

Now he should have played 7. P×P, and if 7. ...., Q×P;
8. Kt—B3, developing with gain of time. Or if 7. ...., Kt×P;
8. B×B, K×B; 9. Q—B1, P—Kt3; 10. Q—Kt2 ch, K—Kt1;
11. Kt—B3, when White has chances of attack on both wings.

7. ....   Kt—B3
He should have played 7. ...., P—Q5 at once, since the
variations given in the preceding note would still have been
playable on White's eighth move.

8. Q—B1
(A pointless move. It places the Queen on an inferior square,
where she plays no part in White's defences.)
Yes; now this move, which would have been good in the
variations mentioned above, is very bad and out of place, since
the White Queen is decentralised for no good reason.

8. ....   P—Q5
9. P—Q3
P—K3 is no longer effective, since Black could reply, as he
does in the game, with P—K4, when he threatens an eventual
P—K5.

9. ....   P—K4
(Weak; it cuts down the Bishop's diagonal and weakens
KB3 and Q3.)
I cannot agree with this. P—K4 is far from being a weak
move for Black. It gives him a stronger hold on the centre and
does not really obstruct the KB so very much. In fact, it acts as a
kind of spearhead for that piece, and the pawn and Bishop in
conjunction provide Black with extra force and pressure on the
centre. As for weakening of the squares Q3 and KB3, this is
of no practical importance, since White has no means of
striking at these supposedly weak squares.

10. QKt—Q2   R—K1
11. Kt—K1
(The idea of hypermodern chess is to allow the opponent to
occupy the centre and then blast him out. Here White cannot
do this without being smashed—which is exactly what happens.)

The trouble for White is that he has allowed Black to get much too strong a hold on the centre. The idea of hyper-modern chess is to allow the opponent to occupy the centre in such a way as to permit of a strong counter-attack by the hypermodern player. For this purpose, it is essential that the opponent should not have been allowed to establish himself too firmly in the centre; so here the right time to counter-attack was on moves 7 or 8. Now it is too late. The moral of all this is that timing is everything in these hypermodern variations.

11. ....   Q—B2
(To discourage P—B4.)
12. P—K4
(Now the other Bishop is just a looker-on.)
Both here and later on White shows a criminal disregard for the nature of his pawn structure. Since pawns, alas, cannot be moved backwards, one must be specially careful when moving them in the first place. Unlike mistakes with other pieces, errors with pawns cannot be rectified.

The pawn move is bad for the reason given in brackets. Correct is 12. Kt—B2, with two possible plans in view: an assault on the Queen-side by P—QR3 and P—QKt4, or an attack in the centre by P—K3.

12. ....   B—Kt5
(With the threat of B—K7.)

13. P—B3
(If White intended P—B4, then why not immediately?)
Because Black has a won game after 13. P—B4, P×P; 14. P×P, B—R3.

13. ....   B—Q2
14. P—KR3
(Unnecessarily weakening his King-side.)
A disastrous move that should never have entered White's head. Possibly he had in mind the playing of P—B4 without allowing Black's Bishop to return to Kt5 and without permitting Kt—KKt5. But he should have paid attention to the unfortunate KKtP, which is strong enough whilst there exists a

pawn on KR2, but which becomes the weakest point on the board after this move. Little wonder that White's position now rapidly crumbles to pieces.

Best was still 14. Kt—B2.

14. ....   Kt—KR4
15. K—R2   B—R3
16. P—R3

(White "counter-attacks" in vain. Note the contrast in mobility between White's and Black's Bishops.)

16. ....   Q—R4

(Without a piece having been captured, White is helpless.)

White is paying the penalty for far too many pawn moves. Consider how much happier he would now be feeling if he had not *fianchettoed* Queen-side and if his Queen-side pawns were still unmoved. With pawns on QR2 and QKt2 and a Bishop on QB1, he would have some chance of combatting Black's pressure.

17. R—B2   Q—Kt3

(The stage is set for the execution.)

A fine move that appears to threaten B×Kt followed by Q×P; but in reality it is a preparation for switching his Queen over to the King-side for the final attack.

18. R—Kt1

(Hoping for 18. ...., B×Kt; 19. R×B, Q×P; 20. B×P.)

97

18. .... Kt×P

(Devastating. If 19. K×Kt, B—B5 ch; 20. K—R4, P—Kt4 ch; 21. K—R5, Kt—Kt5, followed by mate.)

19. P—Kt4   Kt—Q1
20. B—KR1   Q—K3

(Threatening 21. ...., Q×P ch; 22. K—Kt1, Q×B mate.)

21. K—Kt1

(Suicide. But B—Kt2 is not much of an alternative. The rest is slaughter.)

If 21. B—Kt2, B—B5; threatening Kt—K7 dis. ch. And if then 22. K—Kt1, B—K6.

21. ....   B—K6
22. Q—Q1   Kt×B
23. P×P   Kt×R

Resigns.

A good lesson in the waste of time resulting from too many pawn moves. Out of a game of twenty-three moves, White made ten pawn moves, whereas Black made only five!

From what I have written at the beginning of this chapter and from the excellent quality of the two games given above you can see that we have progressed quite a way in this country in the matter of giving opportunities for boys and girls to take an active part in chess life. In fact, few countries, if any, have so many well-organised junior tournaments. I have written "if any"; but I must admit I now have my doubts as regards Russia, where the organisation for boys and girls chess is very strong indeed.

What is certain is that we lag behind the U.S.S.R. in the field of organised instruction to young players of both sexes. On my visits to Russia I have always been impressed by the great opportunities given to young players to learn how to play good chess. In the Central Chess Club in Moscow, for example, there are regular talks and courses on chess on certain days in the week at which hundreds of boys and girls receive instruction from such famous masters as Levenfish and Konstantinopolsky. No wonder that Russia continues to produce such a flood of great young players!

In this country we have attempted to make some sort of start with such talks; but on a very limited scale, and we shall have to do much more in the future.

All the same, I do not want to give the impression that Russian schoolboys are naturally more gifted for chess than British boys; they have the same defects and virtues as our own —to start off with; but the better teaching does make a difference.

During the period that I was in Russia in 1957, acting as judge at the World Championship match between Botvinnik and Smyslov, I had the chance to see for myself just how good the Russian schoolboys were at chess. I was asked to give a simultaneous display against eleven picked schoolboys whose ages ranged from thirteen to seventeen years at the Central Chess Club in Moscow. Remembering that a predecessor of mine who had visited Russia in 1951 had the mortifying experience of losing twenty games and drawing ten games out of thirty played against Russian boys I resolved to play my very best in an attempt to gain a result that would be a little more gratifying to British chess.

After about two and a half hours' play, I won six games, drew four and lost one. Every game, however, was hard-fought, and here is a good example of one of the games I won.

QUEEN'S GAMBIT DECLINED (BY TRANSPOSITION)
White: H. Golombek. *Black:* L. Barchatov

1.	P—QB4	Kt—KB3
2.	Kt—QB3	P—K3
3.	Kt—B3	P—Q4
4.	P—K3	

Either this or else 4. P—Q4, transposing into the Queen's Gambit, is now necessary, as otherwise Black disturbs White's game by P—Q5.

4.	....	B—K2
5.	B—K2	o—o
6.	o—o	QKt—Q2
7.	P—QKt3	P—QKt3

8. B—Kt2   B—Kt2
9. P—Q4

Transposing into an old-fashioned type of Queen's Gambit that demands great accuracy from both sides. The players both get very similar positions, with the difference that White is always slightly ahead in development, owing to his having had the first move.

9. ....   P—B4
10. BP×P   KP×P
11. R—B1   R—B1

The first inaccuracy. White is now able to give Black what is known as hanging pawns—that is, pawns on Q4 and QB4 that have no support on either K3 or Kt3. In consequence, White can obtain an attack on the weakened pawns. Best is 11. ...., P×P; and if 12. KKt×P, Kt—K5.

12. P×P   P×P
13. Kt—QR4   Kt—Kt3

The second inaccuracy, after which Black is on the slippery slope to disaster. 13. ...., Kt—K5 was still the best move.

14. B×Kt   P×B

He has to submit to the breaking up of his King-side, since after 14. ...., B×B; 15. Kt×P, White wins a pawn with the better game.

15. Kt—Kt2

Not 15. Kt×Kt, P×Kt, when Black's Queen-side pawns have been given much needed support. Moreover, as will be seen, this Knight is destined to reinforce and act as the finishing touch in the attack on the King-side.

As a general rule, one does not want to exchange off pieces when attacking the opponent's King if the latter has a weakness on the King-side. The more numerous the forces one can assemble for exploiting this weakness the better.

15. ....   P—Q5

The best chance, since it helps Black to exchange off some pieces, at any rate.

16. P × P	B × Kt
17. B × B	P × P
18. Q—Q2	R × R
19. R × R	P—B4

Again the best move, since it enables Black to get his Bishop over to defend his King. Note that now 20. Q—R6 would be a dreadful mistake, on account of 20. . . . ., B—Kt4.

20. R—Q1	B—B3
21. Q—B4	Q—Q2
22. Kt—Q3	R—B1
23. Q—R6	Q—Q3
24. P—Kt3	

A useful move with a double purpose. It provides an extra support for the Knight on KB4, and at the same time allows the King a loophole, which in turn means that White can move his Rook off the back rank when he wants to attack.

24.	R—B7
25. R—K1	B—K2
26. Q—R5	R × RP
27. Q × P	Q—KB3
28. Q—Kt4 ch	

Exchange of Queens would give Black excellent drawing chances. Compare the note after White's fifteenth move.

28.	K—R1
29. Kt—B4	

Threatening 30. Kt—R5, and if 30. . . . ., Q—Kt4; 31. Q × Q, B × Q; 32. R—K8, mate.

29.	Q—Kt4
30. Q—R3	R—Kt7
31. B—K4	P—KR3
32. R—R1	P—QR4

Only an apparent defence of the QRP, as White's reply shows.

98

33. R×P   Q—B3

If 33. ...., Q×R; 34. Q×P ch, K—Kt1; 35. B—R7 ch, K—R1; 36. B—Kt6 dis. ch, K—Kt1; 37. Q—R7 ch, and mates next move.

34. R—KB5   Q—Kt2
35. Kt—R5   Q—Kt3

Or 35. ...., Q—B1, when White wins by 36. R—QKt5, followed by Q—B5.

36. R—K5   Q—Q3
37. Q—B5   Resigns

Curiously enough, even after 37. ...., Q—Kt3; 38. R×B, Q×Q: 39. B×Q, Black's King cannot escape from the mating net.

The next day I met my opponent at the World Championship match, and he told me that those boys who had played best against me had been given tickets to come and watch the match.

CHAPTER VII

ILLUSTRATIVE GAMES

HERE is a selection of some master games played in recent years. They have been chosen partly so as to give some practical instruction about the middle-game and partly as a collection of entertaining games for you to enjoy. One thing I do hope they prove, and that is that chess in our time is as bright and interesting as it ever has been in the past—perhaps even brighter. In any case, there are enough beautiful combinations in this last chapter to make up for any passages that may have bored you earlier in the book.

Here is a lesson in that most difficult of all arts in chess, the art of defence. Against an extremely fierce attack conducted by one of the greatest masters of attack that has ever lived, Black keeps his head, strikes back in the centre and eventually triumphs.

GAME NO. 1   ZÜRICH, 1953

English Opening

White:	Black:
P. Keres	V. Smyslov
1. P—QB4	Kt—KB3
2. Kt—QB3	P—K3
3. Kt—B3	P—B4

In the early stages of the game, Smyslov, as second player, is rightly content with holding his own.

The idea of this pawn move is that White must play P—Q4 at some stage if he wishes to gain any sort of initiative, and then Black will exchange pawns and finally play P—Q4 himself with full equality.

4. P—K3	B—K2
5. P—QKt3	o—o
6. B—Kt2	P—QKt3
7. P—Q4	P×P

He must exchange now, otherwise White cramps his game by P—Q5.

8. P×P	P—Q4
9. B—Q3	Kt—B3
10. o—o	B—Kt2

By transposition we have arrived at an old-fashioned form of the Queen's Gambit, in which the White QB is developed on QKt2 rather than on KKt5. The chances are evenly balanced. White's pawns are potentially weak in the centre, but in compensation his pieces have good play.

11. R—B1   R—B1
12. R—K1   Kt—QKt5

Forcing one of the opposing Bishops off its best attacking diagonal by revealing an attack on the QBP.

13. B—B1   Kt—K5
14. P—QR3

14. Kt×Kt, P×Kt; 15. Kt—Q2, P—B4 is rather in Black's favour.

14. ....   Kt×Kt
15. R×Kt   Kt—B3
16. Kt—K5

The starting-point of an attack which does indeed look most promising, since even the QR is ready to join in.

16. ....   Kt×Kt
17. R×Kt   B—KB3

It is this Bishop that is going to be the key to Black's defence; for not only will it be used to protect the King, but also it will counter-attack on the black squares in the centre (in co-operation with the Queen and Rooks).

18. R—R5

Now he is committed to an assault on Black's KR2; there

was, however, no going back, since, after 18. R—K1, P×P; 19. R×P, B—Q4; Black clearly has an advantage.

18. ....   P—Kt3
19. R(B3)—R3

The point of this sacrifice is that after 19. ...., P×R; 20. Q×P, R—K1; 21. Q—R6 with the threat of B—Q3, would seem to force 21. ...., B—Kt4; and then 22. R—Kt3, P—B3; 23. P—KR4 leaves White with a winning attack.

19. ....   P×P

As a matter of fact, had Black wished for a draw, he could now have played 19. ...., P×R; after all; e.g. 20. Q×P, R—K1; 21. Q—R6, P×P; 22. P—Q5 (if 22. P×P, B—K5); 22. ...., B×B; 23. R—Kt3 ch, K—R1, and White has nothing better than a draw by repetition of moves, with 24. R—R3, K—Kt1; 25. R—Kt3 ch, etc. But now Smyslov is playing for the win.

20. R×P

If 20. P×P, P×R; 21. Q×P, B—K5.

20. ....   P—B6!

Since White cannot play 21. B×P on account of 21.

...., R×B; 22. R×R, K×R, Black now gains control of the vital Q5 square and uses it henceforth as a pivot both for attack and defence.

21. Q—B1   Q×P!

To show how tricky the defence still is, if now 21. ....., P×B; 22. Q—R6, Q×P; 23. R—Kt7 ch, B×R; 24. Q—R7, mate.

22. Q—R6   KR—Q1

White was threatening the same combination as given in the last note, but Black has time to free his KB square for the King whilst piling up the pressure on the Queen file.

23. B—B1   B—Kt2
24. Q—Kt5   Q—B3
25. Q—Kt4   P—B7
26. B—K2   R—Q5

White must now play P—B4, since 27. Q—Kt3 would lose after 27. ...., R—Q8 ch; but the text opens up a diagonal that makes this check equally fatal no matter where the Queen is.

27. P—B4   R—Q8 ch!
28. B×R   Q—Q5 ch
Resigns.

Chasing after a pawn in the early stages of the game with one's Queen is not a man-œuvre to be recommended; the expense in time and the fact that in capturing the pawn one opens up lines for enemy attack both add up to a formidable total of positional considerations that are usually more important than the mere material gained. Look at the following bright game for an example of all this:

GAME No. 2   ZAGREB, 1955

Queen's Gambit Declined

White: *Black:*

A. Fuderer   B. Milic

1. P—QB4   P—K3
2. Kt—QB3   P—Q4

Now White must choose between a slow form of the English by 3. P—K3 and transposing into the Queen's Gambit, as he does next move; for he cannot allow Black to disturb his QKt by P—Q5.

3. P—Q4   Kt—KB3
4. B—Kt5   B—K2
5. P—K3   o—o
6. R—B1

Usually White plays his KKt out here, but this transposition has little effect, except that it reserves the option of bringing out the KKt to either KB3 or K2.

6. ....   P—KR3
7. B—R4   Kt—K5

Freeing his position by exchanges; this particular method of doing so was favoured and popularised by the great Emanuel Lasker.

8. B×B   Q×B
9. Q—B2

Threatening to win a pawn by 10. P×P, Kt×Kt; 11. Q×Kt, P×P; 12. Q×P.

9. ....   P—QB3
10. B—Q3   Kt×Kt
11. Q×Kt   Q—Kt4?

Instead of this single piece attack, he should continue his development by Kt—Q2.

12. Kt—B3!   Q×P
13. K—K2

White now has ideal attacking chances and threatens immediate disaster by 14. R—KKt1, Q—R6; 15. R—Kt3, Q—R4; 16. QR—KKt1.

13. ....   Q—R6
14. QR—KKt1   P—KB4
15. R—Kt3   Q—R4
16. KR—KKt1   R—B2
17. Q—R3

A strong move that threatens Q—Q6 followed by Q—K5.

17. ....   Kt—Q2
18. K—K1

Before playing Q—Q6 he frees his Knight for action since he will need it for K5.

18. ....   P×P

Allowing the Bishop to join in the attack; but there is nothing Black can undertake. If, for instance, he tries to develop his Queen-side by 18. ...., P—Kt3; then 19. Q—Q6, followed by Kt—K5 is quite decisive.

19. B×QBP   P—B5

So as to free his Queen at any rate; but the pawn move merely spurs White on to deliver the decisive blow. If, instead, 19. ...., Kt—Kt3; 20. Q—Q6, Kt×B; 21. Q—Q8 ch, K—R2; 22. Q—K8, when White's threat of R×P ch is not to be parried.

20. R×P ch!

White is able to bring off this fine combination by reason of the fact that Black's Queen-side is undeveloped.

20. ....   R×R
21. B×P ch   K—R1
22. R×R   K×R

Or 22. ...., Q×Kt; 23. R—Kt8 ch, K—R2; 24. Q—Q3 ch, with mate to follow.

23. Q—K7 ch   K—R1
24. Kt—K5   P×P

Or 24. ...., Kt×Kt; 25.
Q—B8 ch, K—R2; 26.
Q—Kt8, mate.

25. P—B4! Resigns

He has no means (other than giving up his Queen for the Knight) of preventing 26. Kt—B7 ch, K—Kt2; 27. Kt—Kt5 dis. ch, K—Kt3; 28. Q—B7, mate.

A King side *fianchetto* is often a useful weapon, but it must be handled with care, as it may also be a weakening of the King-side that invites an attack. In the next game we see the roles reversed; it is White who has the passive position and Black who at once assumes the attack.

GAME No. 3 MAR DEL PLATA, 1955

Sicilian Defence

White: *Black:*

L. Pachman   M. Najdorf

1. P—K4   P—QB4
2. Kt—QB3   P—Q3
3. P—Q3   Kt—QB3
4. P—KKt3   Kt—B3

At Amsterdam in 1954 Najdorf played against the same opponent 4. ...., P—KKt3; 5. B—Kt2, B—Kt2; 6. B—K3, Kt—B3;

7. Q—B1, P—KR4; 8. P—KR3, R—QKt1; 9. P—B4, Kt—Q2, but White had the better position after 10. P—QR4, even though the game eventually was a draw. Hence, instead of developing by a King-side *fianchetto*, Black tries a quicker minor-piece sortie.

5. B—Kt2   B—Kt5
6. KKt—K2

To pin oneself in this way is asking for trouble. Even though it obscures the diagonal for the KB, White should play 6. P—B3, B—Q2; 7. KKt—K2.

6. ....   Kt—Q5
7. o—o?

This provides Black with a Heaven-sent opportunity for attack on the King-side. Better was 7. P—KR3, though Black would still have the advantage after 7. ...., B—B6; 8. B×B, Kt×B ch; 9. K—B1, P—K4; 10. K—Kt2, Kt—Q5.

7. ....   Kt—B6 ch
8. K—R1   P—KR4!

This is much stronger than it was in the Amsterdam game already quoted, since it threatens a mating attack by P—R5.

9. P—KR3?

Since he does not manage to dislodge the Black QB, this pawn move merely constitutes a weakening of his King-side. On the other hand, it is essential to prevent Black from advancing his own KRP, and therefore White should play 9. P—KR4.

9. ....   P—K4

Another strong move that gives Black a hold on Q5 and KB5, and incidentally deprives White's Knight of a good post on B4.

10. Kt—Q5   Kt×Kt
11. P×Kt   Q—Q2

He can calmly leave his Bishop *en prise*, since its capture would result in White being mated.

12. Kt—B3

Or 12. Kt—Kt1, Kt—R7; 13. P×B, P×P; 14. B—R3, Kt×R; 15. Q×Kt, P×B, and Black wins.

12. ....   Q—B4
13. B—K3   P—R5!

Played with that volcanic vigour typical of Najdorf at his best.

14. Kt—K4

If 14. P×B, P×P dis. ch, followed by mate in two moves.

14. ....   B—K2

He wants to prevent either White's Knight or Bishop from coming to Kt5 in order to embark on the final winning combination.

15. P—B4   P×P
16. P×P

Appearances are deceptive; by opening up the KB file, White seems to have relieved his position and even to have placed Black in some difficulty owing to the pin on the Knight, but now the volcano erupts and there comes a devastating sacrifice.

16. ....   R×P ch
17. B×R   Q—R4

The only way for White to avert this mating attack is to give up a great deal of material.

18. Q—R4 ch   K—B1
19. R×Kt   Q×B ch
Resigns

He loses the Queen after 20. K—Kt1, B×R; 21. Q—B2, Q—R8 ch; 22. K—B2, Q—Kt7 ch.

One rash pawn move in front of the castled King can ruin a position that has been built up with great care. This comes out in the following game, in which White spoils an excellent position by moving his KKtP.

GAME No. 4

MATCH, REYKJAVIK, 1955

Petroff Defence

White:	Black:
H. Pilnik	F. Olafsson
1. P—K4	P—K4
2. Kt—KB3	Kt—KB3
3. Kt×P	P—Q3
4. Kt—B3	Kt×P
5. P—Q4	P—Q4
6. B—Q3	B—K2

More usual here is 6. ...., Kt—QB3 or 6. ...., B—Q3, but the text move is not bad.

7. 0—0	0—0
8. R—K1	Kt—Q3

An interesting retreat. The point is that after either P—KB4 or B—KB4 White gets a good attack by 9. P—B4.

9. Kt—B3	P—QB3
10. B—KB4	B—Kt5
11. P—KR3	B—R4
12. B—R2	P—KB4
13. Kt—K2!	

A good move that threatens Kt—B4. He does not fear 13. ...., B×Kt; 14. P×B, since his two Bishops and the fact that he controls the vital K4 square much outweigh the doubled pawns.

13.	P—KKt4
14. Kt—Kt3	B—Kt3
15. Kt—K5	Kt—Q2
16. Kt×B	P×Kt

White, having the two Bishops, now certainly stands better, but now he has the task of getting these Bishops into action.

17. Q—K2	R—B2
18. Kt—B1	Kt—K5
19. P—KB3	Kt—Q3
20. P—B3	

Safe enough, but not the most vigorous; he should play 20. Kt—Q2, with the idea of opening up some lines by P—QB4.

20. ...	Kt—KB1
21. Q—QB2	

Kt—Q2 was still the best move.

21.	Kt—K1

Now Black has had time to manœuvre his Bishop so as to challenge White's QB.

22. R—K2	B—Q3
23. P—KKt3?	

A self-wrecking process that is only to be explained by his desire to retain two Bishops. He should play 23. B×B, Kt×B; 24. QR—K1, when he still has the better game.

23.	Kt—Kt2

Now Black gets busy building up his forces on the King-side so as to profit from the weakness White has created there.

24.	QR—K1	Q—B3
25.	K—Kt2	Kt(Kt2)—
		K3
26.	B—Kt1	R—Q1

Note how Black first centralises his QR before commencing final attacking operations on the King-side. All this phase of the game is a model of its kind as far as Black is concerned.

| 27. | R—Q1 | R—R2 |
| 28. | P—QB4 | |

Setting an interesting trap; if now 28. ...., Kt×P; 29. B×Kt, Q×B; 30. B×P, with advantage to White.

| 28. | .... | P—Kt5! |
| 29. | KBP×P | B×P! |

Now the storm bursts over White's head and Black demolishes his position by a series of most brilliant moves.

| 30. | Kt×B | R×P! |

White cannot accept the Rook sacrifice because of 30. K×R, Kt—B5 ch; 31. K—R2, Q—R5, mate.

31. P×BP

Not the best chance; he could have put up a much better fight by 31. Kt—R5, though Black should still win after 31. ...., P×Kt; 32. K×R, BP×P ch; 33. K—R2, Q—R5 ch; 34. K—Kt2, Q—R6 ch; 35. K—B2, Kt—Kt4.

31.	....	Kt—B5 ch
32.	K—B3	Q—R5
33.	B—B2	

Now the other Knight enters into the game with decisive effect.

33.	....	Kt—R2
34.	R—KKt1	Kt—Kt4 ch
35.	K—K3	R—K1 ch
36.	K—Q2	Kt—B6 ch
37.	K—B3	Kt×R ch
38.	Kt×Kt	

Also hopeless is 38. B×Kt, Kt×R.

38.	....	Q×B
39.	R×P ch	K—R1
40.	Q—B1	R—K6
41.	Kt—B4	R—K8

White resigns.

The lesson to be learned from the following game is that the defending side should not bring his Queen out too early in the game; above all, that the Queen should not be exposed to attack by minor pieces.

GAME No. 5

HASTINGS, 1955–6
Queen's Pawn, King's Indian
Defence

White: *Black*
V. Korchnoi   B. Ivkov

1. P—Q4   Kt—KB3
2. P—QB4   P—Q3
3. Kt—QB3   P—K4
4. Kt—B3

White gets nowhere after
4. P×P, P×P; 5. Q×Q ch,
when the game already has a
drawish appearance.

4. ....   QKt—Q2
5. P—KKt3   P—B3
6. P—K4   P—KKt3
7. B—Kt2   B—Kt2
8. o—o   o—o
9. P—KR3

So as to be able to play
B—K3 without fearing Black's
Kt—KKt5.

9. ....   R—K1
10. B—K3   P—QR4
11. Q—B2   P—R5

12. Kt×RP would be met
by 12. ...., Kt×P.

12. KR—Q1!
One of the difficult points
in the early middle-game is to
settle where the Rooks should
go. This is the right Rook for
Q1, as White wishes to keep
the QR for QKt1, with eventual threats of P—Kt3 or
P—Kt4.

12. ....   Q—R4
As White proceeds to show,
the Black Queen is vulnerable
here. Better is 12. ....,
Q—K2, so to exert pressure
on White's K4.

13. QR—Kt1   P×P
14. Kt×QP   Kt—B4
15. P—QKt4   P×P e.p.
16. P×P   Q—Kt5
Again a bad square for the
Queen; better was Q—B2.

17. B—B4   B—B1
A better defence was 17.
...., R—Q1, though White
would still have had a marked
advantage after 18. Q—Q2.

18. B—Q2
Forcing the Queen to move
once more on account of the
threat of Kt—Q5.

18. ....   Q—Kt3
19. B—K3
And now the threat is
P—QKt4; the Black Queen is
given no peace.

19. ....   Q—Kt5
20. Q—Q2   Q—Kt3
Forced; if 20. .... Q—R6;
21. Kt—B2, Q—R3; 22.
R—R1.

21. P—QKt4   Kt(B4)×P
22. Kt×Kt   Kt×Kt
23. Q—Q3

Leaving Black no choice but to give up his Knight, after which the game is hopeless. For if 23. ...., P—Q4; 25. Kt—K6, P—QB4; 26. Kt × B, R × Kt; 27. P × QP, or if 23. P—KB4; 24. Kt × KBP, and finally if 23. ...., Kt—B3; 24. Kt—K6, Q—R3; 25. Kt—B7.

23.	Kt × BP
24. B × Kt	Q—B2
25. R—K1	R × R ch
26. R × R	B—Q2
27. P—Kt5	P—R4
28. P × P	P × P
29. Kt—Kt5	

It is fitting that the finishing touch should come from a further attack on the Queen by a minor piece.

29.	Q—Kt1
30. Kt × P	Q × Kt
31. Q × Q	B × Q
32. R—Q1	B—K3
33. R × B	B × BP
34. B—Q4	B—K3
35. B × P	R—QB1
36. P—R4	Resigns

How often one is tempted to chase away a Bishop from pinning a Knight in front of the King right back to Kt3 or K3 by advancing the KKt pawn—and how often this turns out to be a fatal weakening of the King-side! The way to take advantage of such a weakness is beautifully shown in the following game.

GAME No. 6   MARIANSKE LAZNE, PRAGUE, 1956

Alekhine Defence

White:	Black:
Ragosin	Sefc
1. P—K4	Kt—KB3
2. P—K5	Kt—Q4
3. P—QB4	Kt—Kt3
4. P—Q4	P—Q3
5. P × P	KP × P

Better than 5. ...., Q × P; 6. P—B5, Q—K3 ch; 7. B—K2, Kt—Q4; 8. Kt—QB3 with a clear advantage for White. But Black may also play 5. ...., BP × P, with about a level game.

6. Kt—QB3   P—KKt3

An idea introduced by the leading Soviet authority on this defence, Mikenas, in order to put pressure on White's Q4. This game, apart from its worth later on, is also of theoretical value in showing that the older 6. ...., B—K2 is preferable.

7. Kt—B3   B—Kt2
8. B—Kt5

A clever way of inducing Black to spoil his King-side pawn formation.

8. ....   P—KB3

If 8. ...., Q—Q2; then, not 9. Q—K2 ch, Q—K3; 10. Kt—Kt5, Kt—R3, which gets White nowhere, but 9. P—B5, P×P; 10. P×P, Q×Q ch; 11. R×Q, Kt(Kt3) —Q2; 12. Kt—Q5, and White wins.

9. B—K3   P—B3

There was certainly no need to play this pawn move, and instead Black should have simply castled.

10. P—QR4   B—Kt5

Black is unlucky in his choice of moves. Whereas a moment ago it was wrong to move a pawn, now it is bad to move a piece. He should have stopped White's Queen-side advance by 10. ...., P—QR4.

11. P—R5   Kt—B1
12. Q—Kt3   Q—B2
13. B—K2   o—o
14. o—o   K—R1
15. B—B4

Another cunning move that threatens P—B5 and invites Black's KKtP to advance.

15. ....   P—KKt4?

Black seems only too willing to be tempted. He is clearly tired of the cramped position and is striving for room at all costs; but the costs are too

great here, and he should have contented himself with playing the patient 15. ...., Q—B2.

16. B—K3   P—KR3

Buttressing what he realises to be a weak point; but, curiously enough, the KtP is still not safe.

17. Kt×P!

A remarkable combination that must have been calculated out almost to the end of the game.

17. ....   B×B
18. Kt—K6   Q—B2
19. Kt(B3)×B   Q×Kt
20. Q×P   Q—Q2

Thus Black succeeds in shutting in and capturing the Queen; but it costs him two Rooks and a pawn and also a completely broken pawn position.

21. Q×R   Kt—K2
22. P—R6   Kt×P

The Knight must be given up; otherwise the White Queen escapes by Q—Kt7.

23. Q×R ch   B×Q
24. R×Kt   K—Kt2?

This hastens the end, since by placing the King on the same rank as the Queen he dooms it to be captured by the Rooks. However, even with the best play, 24. ...., Kt—B1 he would have a lost position after 25. Kt—B4, as the Black pawns are too weak and the White Rooks too strong in co-operation.

25. KR—R1	Kt—B1
26. P—Q5	P—QB4
27. P—QKt4	P×P

There is nothing to be done; against other moves White wins by Kt—B4 and Kt—K6.

28. R×RP   Resigns

The art of taking advantage of the opponent's broken pawn position is shown to perfection in the following dramatic game, which was played in the last round of the great Moscow Tournament and decided that the first prize should be shared by Botvinnik and Smyslov.

GAME No. 7

ALEKHINE MEMORIAL
TOURNAMENT, MOSCOW, 1956
Sicilian Defence

White:	Black:
P. Keres	M. Botvinnik
1. P—K4	P—QB4
2. Kt—KB3	Kt—QB3
3. P—Q4	P×P
4. Kt×P	Kt—B3
5. Kt—QB3	P—Q3
6. B—KKt5	P—K3

| 7. Q—Q2 | P—KR3 |

If Black wants to avoid having his pawn position broken up, he must precede this by 7. ...., P—QR3; but Botvinnik hopes for more than adequate compensation in the possession of two Bishops.

8. B×Kt   P×B

Black must recapture this way, for after 8. ...., Q×B; 9. Kt(Q4)—Kt5, Q—Q1; 10. o—o—o, White wins the QP. Note that this variation would not be playable if Black had already played P—QR3.

9. o—o—o   P—R3

Necessary to prevent White's Kt—Kt5.

10. P—B4   P—KR4

Partly so as to have the alternative of developing his KB on R3 or K2, partly so as to prevent White's KB from reaching KKt4.

11. K—Kt1	B—Q2
12. B—K2	Q—Kt3
13. Kt—Kt3	

A strong move that avoids exchanges and maintains pressure on the weak pawns. In a game earlier in the year between Keres and Petrosian at Amsterdam the former played 13. KR—B1, and after 13. ...., Q×Kt; 14. Q×Q,

Kt×Q; 15. R×Q, Black had much less to fear.

13. .... o—o—o
14. KR—B1 Kt—R4

If Black precedes this by 14. ...., K—Kt1, then White has time to bring a Rook into the attack by 15. R—B3, Kt—R4; 16. Kt—Q5, P×Kt; 17. Kt×Kt, with the terrible threat of R—QKt3 (Bivshev-Livshin, Leningrad, 1953).

15. R—B3 Kt×Kt
16. RP×Kt K—Kt1
17. Kt—R4 Q—R2

Black is still obsessed with the idea that the two Bishops constitute his greatest strength otherwise he would have played 17. ...., B×Kt, when, though White has the better game, the presence of Bishops of opposite colour make the draw more likely.

18. P—B5!

A fine move that fixes and lays bare Black's pawn weaknesses.

18. .... B—K2
19. P×P P×P

Now pause and look for the combination.

20. R×P!

This beautiful move wins a pawn and breaks down Black's resistance. If now 20. ...., B×R; 21. Q×P ch, K—R1; 22. Kt—Kt6 ch. Or if 20. ...., B×Kt; 21. R×P, and—the chief variation—if 20. ...., P—Kt4; 21. R—B7, B—K1; 22. R—Kt7, P×Kt; 23. Q—Kt4 ch, K—R1; 24. P—K5, B—QB3; 25. P×P, winning his piece back with a most ferocious attack.

20. .... R—R2
21. R—Kt6 P—Kt4
22. Kt—B3 Q—B4
23. Kt—R2

The further career of this Knight is most remarkable. White's plan is to concentrate his forces against Black's weak KP, so he intends to get the Knight to KB4 via Q3.

23. .... K—R2
24. Kt—Kt4 R—KB1
25. B—B3 P—R5
26. P—R3 B—B1
27. Kt—Q3 Q—B2

If 27. ...., Q—Q5; 28. P—B3, Q—Kt3, and White can choose between his original plan of Kt—B4 and the thrust P—K5.

28. Kt—B4 R—B3
29. B—Kt4 R×R

The KP is lost, however he plays. If 29. ...., R(R2)—B2; 30. Kt×P, B×Kt; 31. B×B, R×R; 32. B×R.

30.	Kt×R	B—Kt2
31.	B×P	B—Q1
32.	B—Q5	B×B
33.	Q×B	R—B2
34.	P—K5	Resigns

For pure artistry in the use of two Bishops the following game would be hard to beat. Though the victim in this case, I enjoyed playing the game, naturally not as much as if I had won it, but still from the point of view of an admirer of deep strategy and logical thinking in chess. In this respect Bronstein stands out as the most original chess strategist of our time.

GAME No. 8

ALEKHINE MEMORIAL
TOURNAMENT, MOSCOW, 1956
Queen's Pawn, Nimzowitsch
Defence

White:	Black:
D. Bronstein	H. Golombek
1. P—Q4	Kt—KB3
2. P—QB4	P—K3
3. Kt—QB3	B—Kt5
4. Kt—B3	

A rather unusual way of treating this defence. White ignores the pin and proceeds with his development.

4. ....   P—QKt3
Another, and safer, method of equalising is 4. ...., P—B4.

| 5. | P—K3 | B—Kt2 |
| 6. | B—Q3 | Kt—K5 |

And now 6. ...., P—B4, as Bronstein himself played in his 1951 World Championship match against Botvinnik, seems preferable.

7. o—o   B×Kt
I played this, fully aware of the dangers of two Bishops in such a position, but hoping for counterplay against White's QB pawns; how Bronstein nullifies this is very instructive.

Capturing the pawn on QB6 gives White too strong an attack, as was shown in a game Denker–Fine, U.S.A. Championship, New York, 1944: 7. ...., Kt×Kt; 8. P×Kt, B×P; 9. R—Kt1, B—R4; 10. B—R3, P—Q3; 11. P—B5, o—o; 12. P×QP, P×P; 13. P—K4, R—K1; 14. P—K5, P×P; 15. Kt×P, Q—Kt4; 16. P—Kt3, P—Kt3; 17. Q—R4.

8.	P×B	o—o
9.	Kt—K1	P—KB4
10.	P—B3	Kt—KB3

This looks natural enough, but is it the best? What Black must strive to do is to attack the QBP as quickly as possible, and for this purpose the awkward-looking 10. ...., Kt—Q3; was preferable, with

Kt—B3 and Kt—R4 to fol-
low.

11. P—QR4   Kt—B3
12. P—K4   P×P

A better defensive chance
here was P—Kt3, even though
in so playing the King-side
would be weakened.

13. P×P   P—K4

Hoping to induce White, by
putting pressure on his Q4, to
advance the pawn to Q5 and
thus give Black use of the
square QB4. Bronstein, however, is not to be lured into
this positional error, and proceeds with the attack whilst
disregarding such pressure as
Black does obtain on his Q4.

14. B—Kt5   Q—K2
15. Kt—B2

The Knight is bound for
Q5, where, once established
its effect will be devastating.

15. ....   Q—Q3
16. B—R4

A subtle way of parrying
the threat on his Q4; if now
16. ...., P×P; 17. B—Kt3,
Q—B4; 18. P×P, Kt×QP;
19. B—B2.

16. ....   QR—K1
17. B—Kt3   Q—K2
18. Kt—K3   P—Q3

Again the QP cannot be
captured, for if 18. ....,
P×P; 19. Kt—B5, with variations similar to that given in
the previous note.

19. B—R4!

Now the threat of Kt—Q5
becomes acute.

19. ....   Kt—Q1
20. Kt—Q5   B×Kt
21. BP×B

Threatening to win the exchange by B—QKt5. In view
of this, Black's reply is forced,
but it suffers from the great
disadvantage of opening up
fresh lines for White's Bishops.

21. ....   P—B3
22. Q—Kt3   K—R1
23. QR—K1   P—KR3
24. Q—R3

All through the game White
has played with an assortment
of pins, and now the pressure
becomes intense in this direction. He threatens 25. P×BP,
Kt×BP; 26. B—QKt5,
R—B1; 27. P×P, Q×P; 28.
B—Kt3, and therefore Black,
in order to guard his K4, must
weaken his King-side.

24. ....   P—KKt4
25. B—Kt3   Kt—Q2
26. P×BP   Kt×P
27. B—Kt5   R×R ch

Despite the exchange of all
the Rooks that now ensues,

White's pressure continues to increase.

28. R×R   Kt(B3)—Kt1
29. B—QB4   R—KB1
30. R×R ch   Q×R
31. P×P

This gains material, since if 31. ...., P×P; 32. Q×Q ch, Kt×Q; 33. B×P ch.

31. ....   Kt—B4
32. P×P   Kt×KP

Apparently at last one of Black's Knights has obtained counter-play; but this is only seeming, and the end is near.

33. P—Q7!   Kt—B4
Or 33. ...., Kt×QP; 34. Q×Q ch, Kt×Q; 35. B—K5 ch, K—R2; 36. B—Q3.

34. B—K5 ch   K—R2
35. B—Q3 ch   Resigns
Because of 35. ...., K—Kt1; 36. Q—R2 ch. Just look at the final position for a moment and I think you will agree that these were not Bishops, but Archbishops.

Another aspect of the counter-attacking qualities of the Sicilian is to be seen in the next game. Here the question is who shall control the centre; that Black achieves this by an exchange sacrifice is not an unusual process for this type of opening and middle-game.

GAME No. 9

ALEKHINE MEMORIAL TOURNAMENT, MOSCOW, 1956
Sicilian Defence

White: *Black:*
N. Padevsky   M. Botvinnik

1. P—K4   P—QB4
2. Kt—KB3   Kt—QB3
3. P—Q4   P×P
4. Kt×P   Kt—B3
5. Kt—QB3   P—Q3
6. B—QB4   P—K3
7. o—o   B—K2
8. B—K3   o—o

Black runs less risks here if he first mobilises his Queenside and plays 8. ...., P—QR3; 9. P—B4, Q—B2, with an eventual Kt—QR4 and P—QKt4 to follow.

9. B—Kt3   Kt—QR4
The same idea as given in the previous note, but a riskier method, since it abandons control of his K4.

10. P—B4   P—QKt3
And now safer would have been, first, 10. ...., P—QR3, since after the text move White could have obtained a strong attack by 11. P—K5.

11. Q—B3?

Not a good move, since it exposes the Queen to an indirect attack by Black's QB.

11. ....   B—Kt2
12. P—Kt4

After 12. P—B5, P—K4; 13. Kt(Q4)—K2, Kt×B; 14. RP×Kt, Black breaks open the centre to his advantage by 14. ...., P—Q4.

12. ....   R—B1
13. P—Kt5

Anticipating that Black will play Kt—K1 and so relieve the pressure on White's K4; Botvinnik has prepared the exchange sacrifice mentioned at the head of this game.

13. ....   R×Kt
14. P×R

Better would be 14. P×Kt, R×QB; 15. Q×R, B×BP, with about a level game, though Black's two Bishops should prove very powerful in such an open position.

14. ....   Kt×P
15. Q—Kt4   Q—B1

A strong move both in attack (on QB6) and in defence (K3).

16. R—B3

If 16. P—B5, P—K4; 17. Kt—B3, Kt×B; 18. RP×Kt, Q×QBP; 19. QR—K1, P—Q4, followed by B—B4, with great advantage to Black.

16. ....   Kt×B
17. RP×Kt   P—B4
18. Q—R4

Taking off *en passant* leads to the following interesting line given by Botvinnik: 18. P×P e.p., R×P; 19. P—B5, P×P; 20. Kt×P, B—B1; 21. Kt—R6 ch, R×Kt; 22. Q×Q, R—Kt3 ch; 23. K—B1, B×Q; 24. R×P, B—Kt5; 25. R(B3) —B7, B—R6 ch; 26. K—K1, R—K3, with a won game for Black.

18. ....   P—K4
19. R—R3   P—KR3
20. Q—R5   Q×P
21. R—Q1   P×Kt
22. B—Q2

If 22. B×P, Q×BP; 23. P×P, Kt—B3, whilst after 22. P×P, Black discloses his protection of his KKt2 by 22. ...., P×B.

22. ....   Q—B3
23. P×P   Kt—Kt4

23. ...., Kt—B3, would not be so good, on account of 24. Q—Kt6.

24. R—Kt3   Q—R8 ch
25. K—B2   Kt—K5 ch

Resigns

Whilst it is true that the best form of defence is a counter-attack, to start to do so before one has completed one's development is just asking for trouble. This applies even more to Black than to White, since the second player is (or should be) always a little behind in development, anyway.

The next game shows how such a premature attempt should be punished.

GAME No. 10

ALEKHINE MEMORIAL TOURNAMENT, MOSCOW, 1956

English Opening

White:	Black:
M. Botvinnik	L. Szabo
1. P—QB4	P—KKt3
2. P—KKt3	B—Kt2
3. B—Kt2	P—K4

Not a good move at this stage, since it allows White too much control of the white squares in the centre. Better is 3. . . . ., Kt—KB3.

| 4. Kt—QB3 | Kt—K2 |
| 5. P—Q3 | P—QB3 |

Hoping to be allowed to play P—Q4, but White at once sees to this possibility.

| 6. P—K4 | P—Q3 |
| 7. KKt—K2 | P—QR3? |

The idea is to start up a counter-attack on the Queen-side by P—QKt4; but there are two important reasons why he should not play this move: one is that he has not yet done anything about the development of his Queen-side pieces, and the other that White can put a stop to this counter-attack with the utmost ease. Preferable therefore was 7. . . . ., B—K3.

| 8. P—QR4 | P—QR4 |

This looks odd in relation to his previous move, but he does not relish the idea of having his Queen-side crippled by P—R5.

9. B—K3	B—K3
10. 0—0	Q—Q2
11. P—Kt3	P—R4

Another unnecessary pawn move. The indicated line was 11. . . . ., Kt—R3, with Kt—B2 to follow.

12. P—R4	B—R6
13. P—Q4	0—0
14. R—R2!	

One of those deep moves that recur again and again in Botvinnik's games. The first aim is to remove the Rook from the reach of Black's KB, but there is a higher centralising purpose that will become evident on move 19.

14. ....   B×B
15. K×B   P—Q4?

Prematurely opening up the centre before he has completed his development; little wonder that he meets with such rapid and severe punishment. His position is already very difficult, however, and he has an inferior game whatever he does. Best seems 15. ...., R—Q1, and if 16. R—Q2, Q—B2; 17. P×P, B×P.

16. QP×P   P×BP
17. P×P   B×P
18. Q×Q   Kt×Q
19. R—Q2!

A powerful move that demonstrates the faulty character of Black's method of defence and the triumph of White's strategy. Black cannot contest the Queen's file, for if 19. ...., KR—Q1; 20. KR—Q1, and White wins material. He therefore decides to try to relieve his game by exchanges, but is pulled up short in the attempt by a nasty surprise on White's twentieth move.

19. ....   B×Kt
20. R×Kt!

Much stronger than 20. Kt×B, when Black has a good game by 20. ...., Kt—K4.

20. ....   B—Kt5

21. P—B5   KR—K1

Hoping White will content himself with the win of a pawn by 22. R×P, when 22. ...., QR—Q1 would give his pieces a little play.

22. KR—Q1!   P—B4
He cannot defend his QKtP. If 22. ...., QR—Kt1; 23. B—B4, or if 22. ...., R—R2; 23. R—B7, followed by R(Q1)—Q7.

23. R×P   P×P
24. R—Q6   K—B2
25. Kt—B4   KR—QKt1
26. R(Kt7)—Q7   K—K1
27. Kt—K6   Resigns

Kt—B7 with or without check is always fatal, e.g. 27. ...., K—B2; 28. Kt—B7, R—R2; 29. B—Kt5.

It is a good general principle that, when you are confronted with something unusual in the opening, you should consider what bearing this has on the centre. It is in the centre that the main battle in the opening stages takes place and even unusual moves have to take this into account. In the following game, Black, faced with a different plan from normal against the French Defence, neglects to pay attention to the centre—with fatal results.

GAME No. 11
INTERZONAL TOURNAMENT
AT SOUSSE, 1967
French Defence

White: Black:
R. Fischer   Mjagmarsuren
1. P—K4   P—K3
2. P—Q3

The idea of this unusual move is to keep the centre closed, i.e. to avoid exchanging pawns in the centre, and to aim at eventual control of K5. Once this has been established White can go over to the attack on the King-side.

2. ....   P—Q4
3. Kt—Q2   Kt—KB3
4. P—KKt3   P—B4
5. B—Kt2   Kt—B3
6. KKt—B3   B—K2

Black fails to take any action against White's plan and hopes to proceed by simple development. Instead he should have fought for control of his central K4 square by 6. ...., B—Q3; 7. 0—0, 0—0; 8. R—K1, Q—B2; 9. Q—K2, P×P; 10. P×P, P—K4; 11. Kt—B4, Kt—Q5; with a level game.

7. 0—0   0—0
8. P—K5   Kt—Q2
9. R—K1   P—QKt4

Again, he neglects the centre; correct was 9. ...., P—B3; and if 10. P×P, Kt×P; 11. Kt—Kt5, P—K4.

10. Kt—B1   P—Kt5
11. P—KR4

The start of the King-side attack, but also a useful move to safeguard the development of his QB, as will soon become apparent.

11. ....   P—QR4
12. B—B4   P—R5
13. P—R3   P×P
14. P×P   Kt—R4
15. Kt—K3

Inviting Black to play P—Q5 when White will have the ideal central square of K4 for use by his Knights.

15. ....   B—R3
16. B—R3   P—Q5

Black succumbs to the temptation; instead he should have played 16. ...., R—Kt1.

17. Kt—B1   Kt—Kt3
18. Kt—Kt5   Kt—Q4
19. B—Q2   B×Kt

Giving White the advantage of two Bishops; but by now he had no good move.

20. B×B   Q—Q2
21. Q—R5   KR—B1
22. Kt—Q2   Kt—B6
23. B—B6

A powerful sacrifice. If now 23. ...., P×B; 24. P×P, K—R1; 25. B—B5, P×B; 26. R—K7, Q—Q1; 27. R×P, Q—Kt1; 28. Kt—B3, Q—Kt3;

29. Q×Q, P×Q; 30. Kt—Kt5, and Black is helpless against the threat of 31. R—R7 ch, K—Kt1; 32. P—B7 ch, K—B1; 33. Kt—K6 ch.

23.	....	Q—K1
24.	Kt—K4	P—Kt3
25.	Q—Kt5	Kt×Kt
26.	R×Kt	P—B5
27.	P—R5	P×P
28.	R—R4	R—R2

To guard against the threatened 29. RP×P, BP×P; 30. R×P, K×R; 31. Q—R4 ch, followed by mate in two moves.

| 29. | B—Kt2 | P×P |
| 30. | Q—R6 | Q—B1 |

Losing quickly; he still loses, but more slowly, after 30. ...., P—B8=Qch; 31. R×Q, R×R ch; 32. Q×R, as the Black King is in a mating vice.

| 31. | Q×RP ch | Resigns |

Because of 31. ..., K×Q; 32. P×P db. ch, K×P; 33. B—K4 mate. Two Bishops!

Though the following game is between two great players it is instructive to observe that it is won and lost through two quite basic causes. The first is the failure on Black's part to counter-attack as quickly as possible, and the second is the neglect of that hint that I give earlier in the section on the middle-game about taking care of the danger when one's opponent places his Rook opposite your Queen.

GAME No. 12
7TH MATCH GAME CANDIDATES' FINAL AT KIEV 1968

Queen's Pawn, King's Indian Defence

White:	*Black:*
B. Spassky	V. Korchnoi
1. P—Q4	Kt—KB3
2. P—QB4	P—KKt3
3. Kt—QB3	B—Kt2
4. P—K4	P—Q3
5. P—B3	o—o
6. B—K3	Kt—B3

Or he may play 6. ...., P—K4 at once, as given in the line on page 77

7.	KKt—K2	P—QR3
8.	Kt—B1	P—K4
9.	P—Q5	Kt—Q5
10.	Kt—Kt3	Kt×Kt
11.	Q×Kt	P—B4

To prevent White from playing P—B5, but correct was the immediate counter-attack by 11. ...., Kt—R4 and 12. ...., P—KB4.

| 12. | P×P e.p. | P×P |
| 13. | o—o—o | B—K3 |

And now he should have removed his Queen from the Q file by 13. ...., Q—K2.

14. Q—R3   Kt—K1
15. P—R4   P—B3

With the idea that if White plays P—R5 he can by-pass the pawn attack by P—Kt4. Nevertheless he clearly weakens his King-side by the pawn move.

16. P—B5   R—B2
17. Q—R4   Q—B2
18. B—QB4   B × B
19. Q × B   B—B1
20. P—R5   QP × P

A little illogical. Although he would have weakened himself on the White squares, he should have played 20. ...., P—Kt4.

21. P × P   P × P
22. Q—K6   R—Q1

Allowing White too much play along the open central file. Better was 22. ...., Kt—Q3 followed by R—K1.

23. R × R   Q × R
24. R—Q1   Q—K2
25. Q × QBP   Kt—B2
26. Q—Kt6

Not at once 26. Kt—Q5, on account of 26. ...., Q—K3.

26. ....   K—Kt2
27. Kt—Q5   Q—K3
28. B × P   B × B
29. Q × B   Kt—Kt4
30. Q—K3   Q—B3 ch
31. K—Kt1   Kt—Q5
32. R—QB1   Q—Kt4

Or 32. .... Q—Q3 when White forces Black to weaken himself on the King-side by 33. R—R1, P—Kt4.

33. Kt—B7   Q—K7

Allowing White to finish off the game very prettily; better was 33. ...., Q—Kt3; though White would still be winning after 34. Kt—K8 ch, K—B1; 35. R—B8, K—K2; 36. Q—R3 ch.

34. Kt—K6 ch   K—R2
35. Q—R6 ch   Resigns

It is a fundamental rule that one should only attack or counter-attack when one has developed and assembled sufficient forces to make the assault really significant. Any attempt at attack without adequate forces merely brings down upon the head of the attacker a just retribution in the shape of a rapid loss. A good example is the following game which was awarded the chief brilliancy prize at the tournament in which it was played.

GAME NO. 13
PUERTO RICO INTERNA-
TIONAL TOURNAMENT, 1969
Sicilian Defence

White: *Black:*
L. Kavalek   M. Damjanovic
1. P—K4   P—QB4

2. Kt—KB3   Kt—QB3
3. P—Q4   P × P
4. Kt × P   Q—B2

Such an early development of the Queen is not advisable; better is 4. . . . ., P—K3.

5. Kt—Kt5   Q—Kt1
6. P—QB4   P—K3
7. P—B4   P—QR3
8. Kt(Kt5)—B3   Q—R2

Again he fails to develop his minor pieces; 8. . . . ., B—B4 was better than the Queen move.

9. P—QR3   B—B4
10. B—Q3   P—Q3

10. . . . ., B—Kt8 looks strong but then, after 11. Q—Q2, B × P; 12. Q—KB2, Black loses a piece.

11. P—QKt4   B—K6
12. R—R2   Kt—B3
13. R—B1   P—KR4

A counter-attack based on insufficient development. Instead he should try to gain command of the central Black squares by 13. . . . ., P—K4, a move which would also help his Queen-side development.

14. B × B   Q × B ch
15. R—K2   Q—Q5
16. R—Q2

A strong move; suddenly Black finds himself in trouble on the Q file. The threat is to win the QP by playing B—K2.

16. . . . .   Q—K6 ch
17. B—K2   Kt × KP
18. R—Q3   Kt × Kt
19. Kt × Kt   Q—R2
20. R × P   Q—K6

Black repeats his positional error; he should have developed his K on K2.

21. R—Q3   Q—Kt3
22. Kt—K4   O—O

Castling into a fierce attack, but he no longer has a safe continuation.

23. Kt—B6 ch   K—R1

After 23. . . . ., P × Kt; 24. R—Kt3 ch, K—R2; 25. B—Q3 ch, K—R3; 26. R—R3 gives White a mating attack.

24. B × P   P—Kt3

This meets with a devastating reply, but so too does 24. . . . ., R—Q1; 25. B—Kt6! when Black gets mated.

25. B × P   P × B
26. P—QB5   Q—Kt4
27. R—R3 ch   K—Kt2
28. R—R7 ch   K × Kt
29. Q—R1 ch   P—K4
30. P × P db. ch   K—K3
31. R × R   Kt × KP
32. Q—R2 ch   Kt—B5

The alternative is 32. . . . .,

Q—B5 when White wins by
33. ...., R—K8 ch, K—B3;
34. Q×Q, Kt×Q; 35. R(R7)
—R8, winning a piece.

33.	R—B4	K—Q4
34.	Q—K2	B—B4
35.	Q—Q1 ch	K—B3

If 35. ...., K—K4; 36.
R×Kt, Q×R; 37. Q—Q6 ch,
K—K5; 38. R—R4 ch. Now,
however, he is mated.

| 36. | Q—B3 ch | Resigns. |

When your opponent is in a
position to open up the centre
at quite an early stage in the
game, it is advisable, even
necessary, to get your King
castled away into safety on the
wing as soon as possible.

GAME No. 14
INTERZONAL TOURNAMENT AT
PALMA DE MALLORCA, 1970
Sicilian Defence

White:	*Black:*
R. Fischer	J. Rubinetti
1. P—K4	P—QB4
2. Kt—KB3	P—Q3
3. P—Q4	P×P
4. Kt×P	Kt—KB3
5. Kt—QB3	P—K3
6. B—QB4	P—QR3
7. B—Kt3	P—QKt4
8. o—o	B—Kt2

If Black wants to avoid the
ensuing complications and get
get his King into safety he
should hasten to castle and
play 8. ...., B—K2 and if
then 9. P—B4, o—o.

| 9. | R—K1 | QKt—Q2 |

Now that Black's QB is
developed on Kt2 he dare not
play 8. ...., B—K2 on ac-
count of 10. B×P, P×B;
11. Kt×KP, when White has
a fierce attack.

| 10. | B—Kt5 | P—R3 |

This, in conjunction with his
next move, results in a quick
loss; better was Q—R4.

| 11. | B—KR4 | Kt—B4 |

Overlooking White's reply;
instead he should have played
11. ...., P—Kt4; 12. B—Kt3,
Kt—K4 when he could still
put up quite a fight.

| 12. | B—Q5 | P×B |
| 13. | P×P dis ch | K—Q2 |

After 13. ...., B—K2 White
wins back his piece with con-
siderable advantage by 14.
Kt—B5.

14.	P—QKt4	Kt—R5
15.	Kt×Kt	P×Kt
16.	P—QB4	K—B1
17.	Q×P	

At the moment White has
only two pawns in return for
the sacrificed Bishop; but his
opponent's King is still much

exposed to attack and the two extra pawns soon display their power by what Nimzowitsch would have called their 'lust to expand'.

17.	....	Q—Q2
18.	Q—Kt3	P—Kt4
19.	B—Kt3	Kt—R4
20.	P—B5	P×P
21.	P×P	Q×P

No better is 21. . . . . ,B×QP; 22. Q—Kt6, threatening P—B6. If then 22. . . . . , Q—Q1; 23. R—K8!

22.	R—K8 ch	K—Q2
23.	Q—R4 ch	B—B3
24.	Kt×B	Resigns

If 24. . . . . , K×R; 25. R—K1 ch, K—Q2; 26. Kt—Q4 dis ch with mate to follow; whilst if 24. . . . . , R×R; 25. Kt—Kt4 dis ch wins.

GAME No. 15
6TH GAME OF THE
WORLD CHAMPIONSHIP MATCH
AT REYKJAVIK, 1972

Queen's Gambit Declined

White: *Black:*

R. Fischer   B. Spassky

1.	P—QB4	P—K3
2.	Kt—KB3	P—Q4
3.	P—Q4	Kt—KB3
4.	Kt—B3	B—K2
5.	B—Kt5	o—o
6.	P—K3	P—KR3

7.	B—R4	P—QKt3
8.	P×P	Kt×P
9.	B×B	Q×B
10.	Kt×Kt	P×Kt
11.	R—B1	B—K3
12.	Q—R4	P—QB4
13.	Q—R3	R—B1
14.	B—Kt5	

All up to here is the regular line of the Tartakower Variation as given on page 75. Now, instead of B—K2, Fischer introduces a new move designed to hinder the development of Black's Queen-side pieces.

14.	....	P—R3
15.	P×P	P×P
16.	o—o	R—R2

Preferable to this rather artificial move is 16. . . . . , Q—Kt2.

| 17. | B—K2 | Kt—Q2 |

Although 17. . . . . , P—B5 gives White the strong post of Q4 for his Knight, this would have been better than submitting himself to this constant pressure. For then, after 18. Q×Q, R×Q; 19. Kt—Q4 he could have challenged the Kt by 19. . . . . , Kt—B3.

19.	Kt—Q4	Q—B1
10.	Kt×B	P×Kt
82.	P—K4	

A typical Fischer move; he has a wonderful capacity for making a position come alive and for creating continual dynamic possibilities for attack.

20.	P—Q5
21. P—B4	Q—K2
22. P—K5	R—Kt1
23. B—B4	K—R1
24. Q—R3	Kt—B1

Or 24. ...., R×P; 25. B× KP, Kt—Kt3; 26. P—B5, when White has an irresistible attack on the King-side.

25. P—QKt3	P—QR4
26. P—B5	P×P
27. R×P	Kt—R2
28. R(B1)—B1	

28. R—B7 would be a mistake on account of 28. ...., Kt—Kt4.

28.	Q—Q1
29. Q—Kt3	R—K2
30. P—KR4	

Depriving the Knight of the KKt4 square.

30.	R(Kt1)—Kt2
31. P—K6	R(Kt2)—B2
32. Q—K5	Q—K1
33. P—R4	Q—Q1
34. R(B1)—B2	Q—K1
35. R(B2)—B3	Q—Q1

Black can do nothing except to wait and see where the attack will fall.

36. B—Q3	Q—K1
37. Q—K4	

Threatening R—B7.

37.	Kt—B3

If 37. ...., R×P; 38. R—K5 and wins.

38. R×Kt	P×R
39. R×P	K—Kt1
40. B—B4	K—R1
41. Q—B4	Resigns

Fischer afterwards said that had Black played 41. ...., K—Kt1 he intended replying 42. Q×RP.

One should never start a game of chess with the idea of playing for equality and securing the draw. That way lies the loss rather than the draw, since if you play for the draw you abandon the initiative and inspire your opponent with the confidence that he is certain to gain the upper hand. Then it is he who has the initiative, whether he has the White or the Black pieces, and you only make the game more difficult for yourself.

Consider the following game in which the Dutch player aims at a draw from the very start.

GAME NO. 16
FROM THE JUNIOR
WORLD CHAMPIONSHIP
AT THE TEESIDE, 1973
Queen's Pawn, King's Indian
Defence

White:	Black:
R. Dieks	A. J. Miles
1. P—QB4	P—KKt3

2. Kt—KB3	B—Kt2	16. R—Q1	Q—R4
3. P—Q4	Kt—KB3	17. P—Kt3	Kt(B5)—
4. P—KKt3	o—o		K4
5. B—Kt2	P—Q4	18. Q—Kt2	Kt×Kt ch
6. P×P		19. B×Kt	Q—K4

White pursues a policy of playing for the draw, hence the pawn exchange and his continual search for equality. But the net result is that the initiative soon passes into Black's hands.

20. QR—B1

Exchange of Queens by 20. Kt—R4, Q×Q; 21. Kt×Q, would leave Black firmly in control of the position after 21 ...., Kt—Kt5.

6.	Kt×P	20.	Kt—Q5
7. o—o	Kt—QB3	21. B—Kt2	B—Kt5
8. P—K4	Kt—Kt3	22. P—B4	Q—B3
9. P—Q5		23. P—K5	

He has no other move since he cannot support the centre by 9. B—K3, without yielding Black the advantage of two Bishops after 9. ...., Kt—B5.

23. R—Q2, Kt—B6 ch; 24. B×Kt, B×B leaves White very weak on the White squares.

9.	Kt—R4	23.	Q—Kt3
10. Kt—B3	P—QB3	24. Kt—Q5	
11. P×P	Kt×P		
12. B—B4	B—K3		
13. Q—B1	Kt—B5		
14. B—R6	R—B1		

This accelerates the end and allows Black to bring off a very pretty finish; but in any case he was positionally lost by now.

A fine move that places the Rook opposite the Queen and foreshadows an attack on the Black squares. Bad would be pawn-grabbing by 14. ...., B×B; 15. Q×B, Kt×P on account of 16. Kt—KKt5.

24.	Kt—K7 db ch
25. K—R1	Q—B7
26. R×R	R×R

Black could also have won by 26. ...., Kt×P ch; 27. P×Kt, Q×Q, but he has an even prettier and more drastic finish in mind.

15. B×B	K×B

27. Q—Q2   B—B6   30. P×Kt, Q×Q etc.
28. Kt—K3   R—B8

29. B×B   29. ....   Q—Kt8 ch
  Allowing a neat mate; if   Resigns
instead 29. R×R, Kt×P ch;

SUGGESTIONS FOR FURTHER READING

Openings

Griffith & Golombek, *Pocket Guide to the Chess Openings* (a succinct selection of the best lines for White and Black in tabular form).

Korn, *Modern Chess Openings*, eleventh edition (present-day theory on all the openings in tabular form).

Levy & Keene, *How to play the Opening* (gives the main lines in run-on form together with explanation and comments).

Sokolsky, *The Modern Openings in Theory and Practice* (an enjoyable work that shows the influence of the opening on the middle-game and even on the ending).

Middle-game

Nimzowitsch, *My System* (a remarkable and original book which should, however, be used more to study middle-game tactics rather than strategy).

Keres & Kotov, *The Art of the Middle Game* (Paul Keres is especially fine on how to analyse).

Pachman, *Modern Chess tactics. Pieces and Pawns in Action* (exactly as described in the title).

Renaud and Kahn, *The Art of Checkmate* (classifies the various methods of mating which are indeed more varied than you might think).

Vukovic, *The Chess Sacrifice* (a fine work that not only classifies the types of sacrifice but reveals to you the possibilities of sacrifice in a vast number of positions).

Endings

Averbakh, *Chess Endings: Essential Knowledge* (everything that the improving player should get to know about this essential phase of the game).

Fine, *Basic Chess Endings* (more for reference than continuous study).

Hooper, *Pocket guide to Chess Endgames* (like the *Pocket Guide to the Chess Openings* this deals with all the main lines of its subject and uses concrete examples to illustrate most lucidly and entertainingly, the chief principles of the ending).

Game Anthologies
Reti, *Masters of the Chessboard* (a wonderful study of the great players of the past with illustrative games).

Individual Game Collections
Alekhine, *My Best Games of Chess, 1908–23* (probably the best collection of games by any one player, and a rich mine of ideas).

Fischer, *My 60 Memorable Games* (chess such as only Bobby Fischer could play and an excellent insight into the way the mind of a grandmaster works).

Golombek, *Capablanca's Best Games of Chess* (Capablanca's games are the best models for the young and aspiring player to follow).

Smyslov, *My Best Games of Chess 1935–1957* (a fine collection of games full of deep strategy).

General
Capablanca, *Chess Fundamentals* (sound and clear as one would have expected).

Reti, *Modern Ideas in Chess* (the best book ever written on chess).

INDEX